DATE DUE

BEETHOVEN STUDIES

BEETHOVEN STUDIES

BY

LUDWIG MISCH

UNIVERSITY OF OKLAHOMA PRESS : NORMAN

BOOKS BY LUDWIG MISCH

Beethoven Studies (1953)
(TRANSLATED BY G. I. C. DE COURCY)

Beethoven-Studien (1950)

Johannes Brahms (1922)

LIBRARY OF CONGRESS CATALOG CARD NUMBER: 53–8813

Copyright 1953 by the University of Oklahoma Press, Publishing Division of the University. Composed and printed at Norman, Oklahoma, U. S. A., by the University of Oklahoma Press. First Edition.

To
my wife

Preface

THE ESSAYS comprising the present volume were written as separate articles and appeared at different times and in various publications, the greater part of them, in the words of Beethoven, *inter lacrimas et luctum;* that is, during brief respites between the horrors of the Nazi period in Germany. Their collection here in book form, together with several others now published for the first time, finds its justification not only in their common reference to Beethoven, but through a unity of focus in the choice and treatment of the themes that will be immediately manifest to the reader.

With a few exceptions, which will be discussed later, they can be looked upon as parerga or preliminary drafts of essays of a more comprehensive nature which in the long run were never written owing to the pressure and difficulties of long years of the cruelest political persecution. The first three, as studies of the B flat major quartet, Op. 130, are more closely related. And if the third, "Two B Flat Major Themes," takes the form of a Beethoven-Schubert study, it will be found that this comparison with Schubert's style helps to give a clear insight into the characteristic aspects of Beethoven's art. Another thread connects the analysis of "The Grand Fugue" and "The Finale of the C Major Quartet," since both represent contributions to a "great theme" which might perhaps be formulated as "Beethoven's Synthesis of the Sonata and Fugue Principle." Moreover, the analysis of the Grand Fugue, which for the first time elucidated clearly the structural idea of the work, is directly related to "The Problem of the D Minor Sonata," the first of the "Two Comments on the A Flat Major Sonata" and the refutation of an erroneous interpretation of "The Thematic Treatment of the Egmont Overture." All these seven essays are concerned with Beethoven ideas or art forms that have either not been recognized hitherto, or misunderstood. The "Pseudo and Riddle Canons" is an examination and discussion of these charming plays on notes, which were one of the Master's relaxations. "Annotations on Some Pianoforte Sonatas," which is written in nontechnical style, is also fundamentally a study in form. And behind the question, "Why did Beethoven Write the Fourth Overture to Fidelio?" we find the problem of form in the higher sense of the "unity of the whole." The discussion of "The Battle of Victoria," which falls a little outside the designated framework, is an excerpt from a lecture on "The Unknown Beethoven."

The last three essays are distinct in themselves. The new interpretation of Beethoven's annotation, "The Upper Pitches of the Voices More Through the Instruments," seemed related to the general theme, and "Non si fa una cadenza" was included because its appeal to the executant musician is still not altogether untimely. Special considerations, however, dictated the choice of the essay "Fidelio: an Ethical Confession," and prompted me to place it at the end. It differs admittedly in theme and treatment from the others, but I hope nevertheless that it will prove not entirely anticlimactic. The original version was written in simple, popular style to prepare a tormented and spiritually depressed audience for a performance of the opera, but only a part of it appeared at that time, and this was restricted even then to a very small circle of readers—the holders of Jewish identification cards—besides being mutilated by the censor. In addition, the "actuality" of this Beethoven opera seemed a further reason to renew the homage to Beethoven's humanity. Here the word "renew" is not entirely a misnomer, since both this essay and "Non si fa una cadenza" have undergone such a thorough revision for this work that they can be considered entirely new articles as compared with the originals.

As already indicated, a certain relationship between the greater part of the themes also prescribed their manner of treatment. However, there was no fixed method behind this, since the perceptive attitude followed no inflexible pattern, but in each instance arose out of the nature of the material itself. The choice and treatment of the themes were conditioned rather by a guiding principle: the conscious effort to comprehend music in its own "dimensions," that is, according to its own concepts in the Beethoven sense of "such questions can only be answered at the piano."[1] This throws the perceptive center of gravity automatically on the side of form.

In instrumental music (and, carefully considered, in vocal music also)[2] form and content are not separable en-

[1] Quoted from memory.

[2] Music for the voice takes its inspiration from the words. It must illuminate them and capture their emotion, not in the sense of a "trans-

tities as they are in poetry and painting. The content, or in ordinary usage, the "matter" or essence of music that is immediately manifest to the musical "understanding"—the artistic feeling—can, in intellectual terms, be grasped symbolically at best. Neither poetic, philosophical, psychological, nor other concepts of extra-musical thought touch the nature of music. But the sensuously perceptive in music is capable of being "understood" and "made understandable" according to musical concepts (for which we have the technical terms peculiar to them) as well as corresponding concepts from other dimensions; that is, form in the broadest sense. This includes everything in the musical process, from the elaboration of the motifs to the movement plan, from instrumentation to dynamics and tempo. Architectural analogies in music, the structure of the whole and the relation of the parts to the whole and to each other, can also be understood and made understandable. This is *form* in the narrower, customary sense. Elucidation of form, in the narrower or wider sense, is investigation of the *specifically musical*, and perception of form is objectively valid perception.

To focus attention on form means nothing less than to disregard, or even deny, the "content." (The essays in question will, I hope, bring out this point.) This springs directly from the consciousness that the content of music is irrational. But such self-restraint with regard to the irrational signifies by no means an impoverishment of the perceptive faculty. For the form (in the works of the great Masters at least) is determined by the content, or rather by the *idea* revealed in it and wholly dependent upon it.

---

lation" but as "supplement," which in its own specific way gives expression to another content than the text, in the words of Richard Wagner to what "is incapable of expression in words."

It is therefore as imbued with life, as individual, genial, and wonderful as the idea itself. And perhaps the study of form is the only way to arrive at a clear perception of the "idea" in the musical art work.

LUDWIG MISCH

New York City, 1953

Contents

These essays appeared previously in the following publications:

1 Annotated Program Note, Berlin Philharmonic Concert (Furtwängler), December 10, 1927

2 *Allgemeine Musikzeitung* (Berlin), No. 37, 1934

3 *Acta Musicologica*, XIII, Nos. I–IV, Copenhagen, 1941

8 *Musikforschung*, 1952

9 *Schweizerische Musikzeitung* (Zürich), March 1, 1938

10 *Allgemeine Musikzeitung*, No. 5, 1935

11 Annotated Program Note, concert by Edwin Fischer, Berlin, June 5, 1930

13 *Allgemeine Musikzeitung*, No. 20, 1920
    No. 13 has been completely revised

BEETHOVEN STUDIES

CHAPTER I

The Grand Fugue

THE Grand Fugue, which is included among Beethoven's last quartets as a work in itself with its individual
opus number, was not primarily intended as an independent composition. Originally conceived as the finale of
the B flat major quartet (Op. 130), it was played for the
first time at the initial performance of this work on March
21, 1825. Beethoven's decision to replace the fugue with
a less exacting finale, even before the work was published,
can hardly be interpreted as a concession to the publisher
and the friendly advisers who did not know what to make
of this tremendous movement. He evidently came to the
conclusion himself that it had grown beyond his original
intentions and greatly overweighted the B flat major quartet. The Grand Fugue had become a world in itself.
Therefore it had to be released from the designed association.[1] But the fact that, to all appearances, it had to re-
linquish its preordained place in the quartet because it did
not meet with general favor, set a stigma upon it, or be-

[1] Only the striking beginning in G major is reminiscent of this
association, since the same modulatory idea is found at the beginning
of the new finale.

came for it at least an evil omen. At all events, only respect for Beethoven protects this work even today from traditional opprobrium.

It is not only considered difficult to understand but actually problematical and has the reputation of being less an inspired than a hyperintellectual work. In a standard biography like Thayer's (40) we read: "It is more a subjectively genial, intellectual work than one springing from the depths of the heart; and it will also scarcely ever touch the heart." Paul Bekker (3), who attempts to interpret the fugue poetically in his work on Beethoven, comes to similar conclusions at the end when he sums it up as follows: "All emotion is stifled. Only speculative perceptions are communicated to the delicately vibrating consciousness." Even Hugo Leichtentritt, who in his *Musical Form* (19) is an out-and-out champion of "this little known and inadequately appreciated work," attributes to it "an almost impersonal, hostile objectivity."

Therefore the Grand Fugue, in its musical evaluation, shares the fate of the final fugue of the Hammerklavier sonata. But while this latter is accepted as a substantial element of the work,[2] the quartet fugue in its splendid isolation can be got round very easily and only now and again some chamber music ensemble undertakes the supposedly ungrateful task of performing it. Even in Beethoven quartet cycles, it is no rare thing to find it omitted.

When one realizes how difficult it was, and how long it took, for the now popular works of Beethoven's last period to make their way,[3] it is fairly obvious to assume

[2] When rattled off in the customary bravura way it only seems to confirm the traditional judgment.

[3] The Ninth symphony, the Mass, the string quartets and pianoforte sonatas as well as the Diabelli Variations.

4

that all that is lacking in the monumental Grand Fugue is —to be understood.

The subject of treatment, once decried as bizarre, no longer seems strange to us, its notorious "roughnesses" no longer an obstacle to its comprehension, and particularly since its daring polyphony never breaks through the logical principles of the harmony, even though at first glance the strange form and complicated structure are confusing. Yet whoever seeks to penetrate into the work will find that it will reveal itself to him. And he to whom it has once been revealed will never again be able to shake off its fascination. He will see that the form is as logical as it is original. He will sense in the ingenious work the sway of an inexhaustible fantasy; and above all, he will be thrilled and moved by a trenchant expressive power that was given only to Beethoven—and to the Beethoven of the last period.

There has been no lack of attempts to popularize the Grand Fugue. Performance by a string orchestra rather than a string quartet seems the most promising method. Hans von Bülow was the first to transfer this mighty chamber music work to the sound dimensions of an orchestra. And Weingartner and Furtwängler followed in his wake.

It rests with the trained musician with a thorough knowledge of compositional technique to fathom the extraordinarily artistic structure of the work in all its details. But the music lover who wishes to carry away a musical impression will also do well to familiarize himself as far as possible with its plan.

The fugue, which is preceded by a special introduction (*overtura*) consists of three main sections along with a coda. Outwardly these three sections,

    a. *Allegro*—4/4—B flat major,

    b. *Meno mosso e moderato*—2/4—G flat major,

    c. *Allegro molto e con brio*—6/8—B flat major,

conform to the movement plan of a sonata (with which Leichtentritt (19) compares them). But only outwardly so, as will be seen on closer inspection. The first section presents the homogeneous theme of the entire fugue linked with a "countersubject" (second theme) and represents a normal and complete double fugue. In the *meno mosso e moderato*, a rhythmically altered version of the (principal) theme is treated fugally, wherein we find a new "counterpoint" which dominates the entire section. The third section, which is framed by a short, marchlike passage and its expanded repetition, brings new developments.[4] However, not only a new rhythmical variant of the theme is worked out here, but the theme itself, broken up into smaller fragments as in a sonata, is also treated fugally. Next comes a section employing the "countersubject" of the double fugue, and finally one that recapitulates the *meno mosso*. The decisive point in arriving at a complete understanding of the form is to recognize that, in the *third* section, the technique of the fugue is merged with sonatalike thematic elaboration. We now grasp in retrospect the secret of the form of the Grand Fugue.

    a. Each section consists of a group of "developments" which unite in Section I to form a complete fugue.

    b. Sections I and II are in contrast. Section III not only presents new elements but draws from the preceding sections. Above all, it combines sonata-form "development"

---

    [4] The term "development," unless otherwise indicated, is used with reference to the fugue, i.e., "progression of the theme through the individual voices."

The Grand Fugue

with fugue-form "developments." *The relationship between the first two sections is that of a first and second "thematic group" (Hauptsatz and Seitensatz).*[5] *The third section bears the same relationship to them as the development section of a sonata.*

This interpretation is further confirmed by the fact that between the close of Section III and the coda, we find quotations from Sections I and II—the sketched suggestion of a recapitulation.

OVERTURA

The *Overtura* forms not only the organic fundament of the entire work, but at the same time an interesting general heading by stating the most important versions of the theme. First, with tremendous emphasis, in heavy *fortissimo* dotted half notes (one to a bar) sounding in three different octaves at once:

EXAMPLE I

[5] (See 41, p. 272). The *Hauptsatz* is the first section of the exposition which establishes the tonic key. It opens with the principal theme (1. *Thema*), but in movements of larger dimension contains more than just the principal theme (the working out of motifs of the principal theme, new ideas, cadences, etc.). It extends to the beginning of the "modulatory part." The *Seitensatz* is the section in the contrasting tonality. It contains (with Mozart and Beethoven but rarely with Haydn) the contrasting second theme (*Seitenthema*), but can likewise contain more than the second theme itself. It extends to the beginning of the closing group (Epilogue or *Schlussgruppe*); that is, in cases in which a closing group is distinguishable as a special section. With Beethoven the closing group usually reverts to the motifs of the principal theme but can also employ new material (as frequently occurs with Mozart). The closing group should not be confused with the coda, which with Beethoven, and at times with Haydn and Mozart also, is the section immediately following the recapitulation.

7

A second version,

EXAMPLE 2

which follows an exciting *fermata*, requires only a simple *forte*, in keeping with its rhythmical movement. The repetition of this theme effects the modulation to F major (the dominant key of B flat) where we now find the third version of the theme with harmonic accompaniment:

EXAMPLE 3

In the repetition, it is counterpointed with the motif that appertains to it later in the working out:

EXAMPLE 4

If here the theme is heard in a yearning *piano* (announcement of the second section), in the fourth version it is stated in a timid *pianissimo*:

EXAMPLE 5

But it is this version that will soon undergo a hard battle in the double fugue, which now begins.

FUGUE

Allegro

(Section I, double fugue). At this point the theme can hardly hold its own against the first stormy countersubject, especially since the other voices powerfully support the rhythm of the countersubject. The conjoined pair of themes runs through the four voices (first development); then a fifth entry of the theme closes the "exposition." A change to E flat major introduces the "modulatory part," which comprises two development sections:

EXAMPLE 6

Owing to the continued *fortissimo* of the conflict between the two themes, an increase in effect (*Steigerung*) can be achieved only by quickening the pace. At the beginning of the second development section, the counterpointed voices oppose the themes with a triplet rhythm. In the third development, the rhythm is even more lively (simultaneously with a rhythmical variant of the theme). In the battle of the episodes the first theme seems to go under completely:

EXAMPLE 7

Only its rhythm maintains itself stoutly against the superior force (bass leaps over three octaves!) but it gains

9

renewed strength and also holds its own against the hostile theme in the fourth development, which brings us to the closing section. In a last rush of excitement, the themes scurry by at redoubled speed, now compressed into two bars as compared with the previous four. Furthermore, the "countersubject" is in triplet rhythm. In the coda the "countersubject" triumphs in the end. But now the picture changes. A modulation to G flat major leads to the

Meno mosso e moderato

(Section II, likewise a double fugue). A motif derived from the (principal) theme

EXAMPLE 8

prepares the entry of one of those wonderful melodies that only the Beethoven of the last period could write. Accompanied harmonically at the beginning, with the above motif eddying round it lightly, the melody is revealed as "counterpoint" to the fugue theme. But this "counterpoint" dictates the character of the entire section, although the fugue theme, in keeping with all the rules of the art, is worked out here:

EXAMPLE 9

In a unison of all four voices, the "counterpoint" then has the last word in this lyrical section of the work.

Allegro molto e con brio

(Section III). The treatment of the fugue theme (in the version shown in Ex. 2) would lead one to believe that a fugue were in the making (entry as dux and comes). But nothing comes of it. A contrapuntal motif is developed freely to a stirring, triumphant marching air round which in turn the theme now eddies contrapuntally:

EXAMPLE 10

We know what marching airs mean with Beethoven. A battle is in the offing. There is an energetic shift from B flat major to A flat major and then the fugue theme in its mightiest form (as it first appeared in the introduction) enters threateningly in the bass:

EXAMPLE 11

Desperate cries answer it,

EXAMPLE 12

and at the same time another call is mixed with it (a motif derived from the theme):

EXAMPLE 13

11

After the first development, the fugue theme breaks to pieces in the battle. Its members continue to fight on independently, the first half during the second development and the second half during the third development with its galloping inrush of triplets. The first violin, which tries to carry the theme above a fearful organ point, trills over a *stretto* of the lower voices, and the triplets, which assume more and more the form of the fugue theme, rush by. The "countersubject" (now changed to 6/8 rhythm) of the double fugue is announced with a soft signal call. A serpent, generated by the theme, hisses back at it:

EXAMPLE 14

The "countersubject," which tests its mettle victoriously in this contest, now crosses swords with the remaining portions of the great fugue theme, which arm themselves for the last battle with a *stretto* of all four voices.

Meno mosso moderato

"Feeling new strength," as it were, the fugue theme now raises its head in a movement corresponding to the first *meno mosso*, though differing from it greatly in character. The soft, delicate G flat major has given place to the lusty energy of A flat major.

Allegro molto e con brio

The return of the march signals the end of the battle. The movement is spun out longer this time. It pauses a moment in mystical reflection and then fades away softly, in a mood of deep spiritual inwardness.

The Grand Fugue

Allegro, meno mosso e moderato

Here we find the aforesaid quotations of the two first
sections, but as already pointed out they have another
sense than the outwardly similar "reminiscence motif"
of the Ninth symphony (aphoristic recapitulation).

Allegro molto e con brio

(The coda). Here the theme is stated in the first version, which is now revealed as the primordial and principal
form, but in an expanded, triumphant configuration in
the bright key of E flat major answered by the quiet 6/8
version of the theme. A mystical mood, over an organ
point (*stretto* in the upper voices)—a breath-taking transition. Triumphant and yearning, joyous and pleading at
the same time, the "countersubject" now surges up in the
octave doubled bass, carried by the first theme and accompanied harmonically by an inner voice. A conclusion
of overpowering majesty and exhalting ethos.

A great deal more might be said about the Grand
Fugue, but only to one who has the wonderful score before him.

CHAPTER II

Alla danza tedesca

BEETHOVEN, as we know, never "repeated" himself. Every one of his creations, with the exception perhaps of certain parerga, works written for special occasions, youthful compositions, and the like, is so individual in character and of such a specific intellectual atmosphere as to make it unique in its class. Nothing is a mere variant of an already existing type. However, it is an entirely different matter when we come to the deliberate use, time and again, of the same theme,[1] to the development of different themes, movements, or works springing from a common thematic germbud,[2] to the repeated preoccupation with the same artistic problem,[3] or to the adoption of the identical, or a related, intellectual idea at different times and in different forms.[4]

Among the examples of the latter is a remarkable analogy existing between two movements dating from

[1] The theme of the finale of the *Eroica* or that of the Turkish March from *The Ruins of Athens*.

[2] The string quartets in C sharp minor and A minor and the Grand Fugue.

[3] The *Opferlied*.

[4] Finale of the *Choral Fantasy* and the *Ninth symphony*.

different creative periods, to which, as far as I am aware, attention has not yet been drawn.

"The souls of great musicians are filled with tonal fantasies, which again and again develop into an art work," wrote Max Graf in his beautiful book, *The Inner Workshop of the Musician*. When he chose the finale of the Ninth symphony to elucidate this thought in detail, he has reference here to such a "tonal fantasy" or "vision" in miniature.

At the head of the first movement of the Sonata, Op. 79, we find the words *"Presto alla tedesca."* At first there is hardly anything to show that the principal theme derives from the German dance. Although written as an eight-bar group, the structure is ametric, not periodic, as is usual for the principal theme of a sonata movement or, as in this case, of a sonatina movement. It does not change to periodic structure (i.e., the structure proper to a dance) until the coda. Beethoven, however, was particularly fond of resuming the principal sonata theme in the coda, so only the title really indicates that the German dance was the intellectual point of departure of this movement. But the origin comes out very clearly in the sketches. The original draft of the theme has a periodic, definitely dancelike form (28, ii; sketches from 1809).

It was only in the further process of creation that Beethoven deliberately changed the dancelike form in favor of a version that seemed to him more suitable for the theme of a sonata movement. But the codalike version proves to be a re-establishment of the primordial form, and looking back at it from the coda, we actually see that the first four bars of the principal theme are really the forephrase (*Vordersatz*) of an originally "periodic" structure.

15

Many years later he returned to the same idea of using the German dance form. As we know, the fourth movement of the B flat major quartet, Op. 130, bears the inscription: *Alla danza tedesca*. In type, this movement is a real dance even though naturally in an idealized form. The similarity of the themes of both movements is very striking.

In so far as the head motif (*Themenkopf*) is concerned, the second theme seems exactly like an inversion of the first. And still, as the sketches show, the theme of the *Danza tedesca* was a new invention and Beethoven only developed it by slow degrees to the configuration we now know (28).

EXAMPLE 15

The point might be raised that this is not surprising since triad themes are not uncommon with him, and in both cases the dance form determined the rhythmic pattern. However, that would be no objection. On the contrary, it would confirm our present contention, namely, that the demonstrably same artistic "vision" characterized by Beethoven himself in an appropriate heading led to a similar artistic "materialization" in creative processes widely separated in time.[5] In spite of the divergencies in

[5] Attention is called to an analogous case with Brahms. Compare the theme of the Lied *Weit über das Feld ein Geier flog* (Lieder, Op. 3) with the theme of the *a cappella* chorus *Der Falke* (*Hebt ein Falke sich empor,*) Op. 93–a. Here we also find a theme springing from the

content, technique, and form, the inner relationships of the two compositions are even closer, as will be seen by comparing the second theme of Op. 79 with the middle portion of the quartet movement.

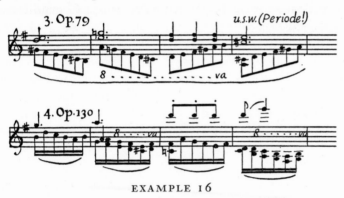

EXAMPLE 16

Furthermore, there is the agreement in key. Anyone at all familiar with the Master's creative processes knows what a distinct character and what expressive value the key had for him—even if indefinable in words. And the sketches show, in addition, that the choice of key was by no means accidental. In the earliest known sketch, the theme of Op. 79 is in C major. The theme of the *Danza tedesca* of Op. 130 was originally sketched in A major, and also worked out in this key, according to Schindler. Schindler and Nottebohm also state that this theme was originally intended for the A minor quartet, Op. 132. In the B flat major quartet, the theme is first stated in B flat major, then to assume its final form in G major. However, the point can always be raised that the movement plan of demonstrably same conception. The flight of the vulture, or the falcon, or more exactly the precipitate ascent of a bird of prey, is symbolized in both instances by a triplet which forms the start for a leap into the highest notes of the melody.

17

the B flat major quartet in its entirety necessitated this new change of key.[6] But even though there were several motives for the final choice of G major, this nevertheless does not nullify the assumption that the concept of the German dance forced Beethoven to return to G major.

[6] See the following essay on "Two B Flat Major Themes."

CHAPTER III

Two B Flat Major Themes

THERE is a striking similarity between the final theme of Schubert's B flat major sonata (post.) and the theme of the last movement of Beethoven's B flat major quartet, Op. 130 (written subsequently to replace the Grand Fugue) which till now has been overlooked although it can help to throw a very interesting light on stylistic and creative-psychological processes.

If we seek the points of similarity in the two themes that tempt the unbiased listener to go into the matter more thoroughly, we find that the correspondence lies chiefly in the harmonic treatment. The actual "melodic" curve— that is, the forward movement in the tonal realm, its motivic structure, its rhythm and meter—is so divergent in the two cases that the Schubert theme maintains its individuality and independence in relation to the earlier Beethoven theme. With Beethoven: thesis. With Schubert: anacrusis. With Beethoven: a large period consisting of two analogous four-bar motif groups. With Schubert: the forephrase of the period consisting of two identical two-bar groups.[1]

[1] Traits of an apparent, merely external, resemblance that should

19

The two themes are so similar in harmonic structure that a family resemblance is unmistakable. Both themes (in B flat major) begin on the (broken) dominant seventh chord on G, which forms a cadence with the subdominant parallel key of B flat major (cc–e^b–g). At the beginning of the afterphrase (also identical in meter) both change from the seemingly remote tonality[2] to the proper, narrower sphere of the principal key, and do so on the dominant of B flat.[3] The fact that the following cadence in B flat major is no longer identical in pattern seems irrelevant in view of the common fundamental harmonic idea.

The similarity is emphasized still more by the single two-bar *g* which precedes both themes. With Beethoven: in melodic octaves. With Schubert: as harmonic octave. In addition, we have the uniformity of accompaniment, the rhythm and figuration of which are identical in both instances. The harmonic treatment with the organ-point-like reiteration of the bass note through the first four bars is also the same except that with Schubert there is an alteration at the end of the fourth bar.

In a resemblance embodied in such original and char-

---

not be overlooked are: With Schubert, the motif ends on the strong beat (*b–c*). This is missing in the afterphrase of the period. With Beethoven, the same feminine ending on the weak beat as motivic link and therefore repeated in the afterphrase (as a–b♭). The sixteenth-note figure in the Beethoven theme is an independent motif. It is therefore found in the forephrase as well as the afterphrase. The sixteenth-note figure in the penultimate bar of the Schubert theme is a melismatic cadential embellishment of typically Schubertian character. See also the following variant of the theme.

[2] From a "functional" point of view, it is here a question of opening with the subdominant, which appears in the independent form of the parallel key, forming a cadence with its dominant, which in turn derives from the altered tonic parallel key. But we will amplify and demonstrate this analysis of the harmonic progression more fully later.

[3] The six-four chord of the dominant, which we find at this point in Schubert, is merely the transcribed dominant.

Two B Flat Major Themes

EXAMPLE 17

acteristic elements, the assumption is justifiable that the
one theme influenced the shaping of the other. Circumstances would indicate that Schubert was familiar with
Beethoven's theme. (The B flat major quartet with the
new finale was performed for the first time in December,
1826, and appears to have been played a number of times

during the following months (40, V, p. 407, 423, 435, 480). Schubert's B flat major sonata was written in September, 1828. Beethoven's final theme may well have re-echoed in his ears in the conception of his own final theme. Naturally one can also assume a duplicity of inspiration. It is unnecessary to mention that in the abstract such an ingenious harmonist as Schubert did not require any external inspiration in order to find his own theme. All that is certain is the priority of Beethoven's.

Still this question, which could be decided definitely only by documentary evidence, is of minor interest in comparison with the vista it opens up to us. A direct comparison of the two themes reveals their common root. We will learn, however, that in Beethoven's intellectual workshop the same harmonic structure has an entirely different significance than in Schubert's realm of fancy.

The stylistic nature of the Beethoven theme can best be grasped from the genetic angle since we can follow the formative process of the theme to its point of departure without referring to direct sketches of the second finale of the B flat major quartet, i.e. (fully aware of the irrationality of the creative act), we can trace the intellectual idea underlying the musical structure of the theme.

A striking feature common to both finales of the B flat major quartet furnishes us our first foothold: the introductory note *g*.[4] The *overtura* of the Fugue begins with a powerful *g* over a span of four octaves, which is still more firmly established by a *fermata* and an octave skip.[5] After this preparation, the theme follows twice in succession in

[4] It is permissible to speak of the "note" *g* for the time being, without any further reference.

[5] As a result of the syncopation and the ties, the octave skip has for the hearer the double importance of sustaining the note and prolonging the opening of the theme with exciting effect.

G major before it passes into the tonic key of B flat major via C and F. What does this mean?

If we consider the Grand Fugue in its present form as an independent work, as Beethoven ultimately intended it to be, it is difficult to find a natural explanation for the G major opening. For that is what it really is. However, as soon as we envisage the work in the place it was originally meant to occupy, the logic of the opening is immediately apparent. The *g* of the *overtura* is the connection link to the last note of the melody of the preceding E flat major movement—to the touching third with which the *cavatina* dies away. It serves as "common note" for a close linking of the movements, for establishing a firmer connection than key relationship alone could effect. The second and third movements of the B flat major quartet, the B flat minor *presto* and the D flat major movement (*andante con moto ma non troppo*) beginning with the B flat minor introduction, are joined in a similar way. But while here the connection involves only a direct modulation to the parallel key, the *g*, which opens the Fugue, changes its function on sounding[6] and becomes at once the point of departure for a highly exciting entry of the final key. The fact that Beethoven employed the same connection device (in an altered form which will be discussed later) in the new final movement shows how highly he thought of it.

Before we can draw conclusions from our findings up to this point, we must examine another detail, which seemingly contradicts our other observations. Contrary

[6] Released from the former bass and extending down into the bass, the *g* will immediately strike the hearer as the fundamental of a new harmony, and this will be confirmed later through the G major of the theme.

to the aforementioned connection links, the intention of which is to guarantee uninterrupted sequence of the movements, the *Danza tedesca* not only dispenses with such a connection link to the preceding movement,[7] but with its G major following immediately on a D flat major section, it even brings two widely remote keys into direct collision.

We know from Schindler and Nottebohm that the *Danza tedesca* was originally intended for the A minor quartet and was sketched out, or even already worked out, in A major. But why was it then transposed to G major when it was taken over into the movement plan of the B flat major quartet, and not to a key (B flat major, for example) related to the keys of the adjacent movements? As a matter of fact, Beethoven considered B flat major while the work was in progress (28, 29), but in the end he rejected it in favor of G major. If we investigate the reasons for this decision, we will be accorded a glimpse into the inner workings of Beethoven's mental workshop.

In the preceding essay on the *Alla danza tedesca*, I tried to show that the idea of the German dance was associated in Beethoven's mind with the key character of G major and that in the B flat major quartet this association was carried through as compellingly as years before when working on the *Presto alla tedesca* of the sonata, Op. 70.

But along with this motif (which the sketches show developed gradually in both instances) we have still another in the *Danza tedesca* that was even more impelling and decisive and shows how absolutely necessary the G major was from the artistic point of view, i.e. the movement plan of the quartet in its entirety.

[7] Here we naturally do not mean to imply that all the movements of Op. 130 should be played straight through without interruption.

Two B Flat Major Themes

Between the compact B flat major complex of the outer movements we find as keys of the inner movements (without the *Danza tedesca*): B flat minor (*presto*); D flat major (*andante con moto*); and E flat major (*cavatina*). If we disregard the key of the subdominant (as traditional for slow middle movements) and take B flat minor as an also customary variant of the tonic key, or also as a parallel key to the D flat major complex, we have the altered D flat major in the second degree of relationship[8] as more remote tonality, which extends the B flat major tonality beyond the ordinary limits. Here Beethoven's wonderful sense of tonality comes into play and lets him bring the most remote keys into organic connection with the tonic key, in accordance with his fantasy and the expression he desires to obtain. In so doing he expands the tonality to a sheerly infinite degree without disrupting it. As counterweight to D flat major, which is necessary in order to maintain the tonal center of gravity, he employs G major, the key which lies equally distant from the tonic center B flat in the opposite direction. D flat major and G major, the keys of the minor third above and below (or the third fifth below and above) represent opposite harmonic poles between which rests the tonic (exactly as between their dominants) as point of departure and goal of contrary, though equally powerful, tensions. Therefore in the texture of the B flat major quartet, D flat major and G major are found one after the other—not irrelevantly but like two dominants of a key (which are also only related through their common relationship to the tonic).

But that is not yet all. The B flat major tonality, extended and given a specific color by the components D

[8] Klatte (15) speaks of a "tonic relation."

flat major and G major, as represented in the key spectrum of the sequence of movements, is already prepared —a microcosm as it were—in the harmonic disposition of the first movement. Here the contrast in key between the *Hauptsatz* and the *Seitensatz*[9] is represented by B flat major and G flat major. And a D flat section, which the *Seitensatz* must pass through before reaching the tonic key, corresponds in the recapitulation to the broad G flat major section of the exposition, which comprises the whole *Seitensatz*, including the epilogue. The development section, however (after two bars of F sharp major, the enharmonic equivalent of G flat major) exhibits the keys D major, G major, and C minor; that is, the two "complementary colors"[10] associated with the harmonic units G flat major and D flat major, and in addition a modulating or pivot key proper to the tonality as transition to the B flat major of the beginning of the recapitulation. If one notes further that the G major section (as regards position and extent)[11] marks the center of the development section and—to a certain extent at least[12]—the culmination point of the modulation curve of the entire movement, then it is immediately clear that the harmonic progression of the first movement shapes the course of the entire tonal structure of the B flat major quartet—that the key quality (color) of the first movement, as defined by

[9] The key of the dominant is already operative in the *Hauptsatz*, special conditions of course being at the basis of this through the contrast *adagio–allegro*.

[10] D major and G flat major, as keys of the fourth fifth above and below B flat, are related to each other as G major to D flat major.

[11] Fourteen bars of G major stand (like a tonic between its two dominants) between ten or twelve bars of D major and nine bars of C minor, the last of which belongs already to the modulating cadence that leads back to B flat major.

[12] Since the return modulation begins with C minor after the G major.

G flat major–D flat major and D major–G major has been projected (simplified, of course) upon the key relationship of the totality of the movements (*Projection ins Grosse*).

Since in Beethoven's art work, as in any living organism, there is a constant intrinsic correlation between the whole and its parts, we can only completely understand one single characteristic feature of the work if we seemingly digress from the given subject and glance at the harmonic structure of the B flat major quartet as a whole. We now know that the G major key in the *overtura* of the grand fugue is something more than a device occasioned by the connecting note *g* and carried into effect by a caprice of fancy in order to introduce effectively the final tonality. This G major is both the consequence and a factor of the stylistic homogeneity of the whole, an ingenious brush stroke which contributes another nuance from the tonality palette of the first movement and movement sequence to the B flat major color of the last movement.[13] It is, so to speak, a last tonal anchoring of the G major of the *Danza tedesca*, which has its first and deepest roots in the G major section of the development of the first movement.

Now we also understand what we formerly could only assert, that is, the value that Beethoven himself attached to this final connection device. And we can therefore go a step further in our conclusions: since this idea was employed in the plan of the finale which was to replace the Grand Fugue, it actually became the thematic germ of the new movement. The idea of passing from the connecting note *g* of the *cavatina* to B flat major (via G ma-

[13] See also the G flat major of the second section (corresponding to a *Seitensatz*) of the Grand Fugue (*meno mosso e moderato*).

jor) guided the inventive fantasy in the conception of the new theme and was transformed into a thematic inspiration.

And if we now investigate the theme once more in this light, we will also discover in it the G major coloring (even though only a hint) which we formerly overlooked. The second harmony, for instance (the clang e–e^b–g over the sustained g) will only be interpreted as subdominant of this key *in retrospect*, from the B flat major. When it first sounds, however, it will be taken for the (minor) subdominant of the tonic G. Proof: the possibility of an easy harmonic progression to the close in G! Whereby it naturally remains an open question whether the beginning aims at pure G major or the "variant" G minor. In the new evaluation of the connection device, the original G major component seems modified to this extent, weakened—if you will—simply to a tonic entry of the G.

But on the other hand is not this modification, the aim of which is to approximate the G major to the B flat major (variant=parallel) a logical result of the compression necessitated by having to adapt it to the disposition of an entirely new composition; instead of the modulating introduction to the Grand Fugue, a "modulating theme" of the finale, a harmonic process carried out previously *by means of the theme* that is now effected *within the theme* itself!

Therefore the final and principal result of this investigation, which lets us spy out the genesis and growth of a Beethoven idea, is the knowledge that the theme of the subsequent finale was derived from the totality of the B flat major quartet, like a new germ cell from a living organism, and that its strange floating harmony with its suggestion of romantic atmosphere (an expression of the sublime humor holding sway in the movement) rests on further consistent, ingenious development of the tonality concept.

If we now try to apply a similar line of reasoning to penetrate the stylistic principle of the Schubert theme, we will go entirely astray. There are no grounds for the assumption—and many against it—that this theme derived from a process of musical reasoning similar to that of Beethoven. A piece in the remote key of C sharp minor (the wonderful *andante sostenuto*) inserted in the otherwise all–B flat major movement sequence of a B flat major work, the free harmony especially of the first movement with its frequent and often rapid change of key, its modulations leading far from the tonic key, and the enharmonic "color spots" scattered along the way—this in itself sufficiently indicates how far away Schubert was here from Beethoven's concept of tonality.[14] And in the previous movements we will seek in vain, for Schubert's final theme, a tonal justification similar to that of Beethoven's. Turning to the first point of agreement—the opening *g*—we find that Schubert's intention was diametrically opposite to that of Beethoven: *contrast* rather than *unification*. After the B flat major close of the *scherzo*, the *g* of the sonata finale, which rings out like a horn blast, has the thrilling effect of the unexpected, giving the impression of a harmonic change of scene, of a new key, while two movements in the same key still follow one upon the other. How very conscious Schubert was of this

[14] As in the B flat major sonata—marvellous as the music is—he is leagues away from Beethoven's idea of the sonata, which he already came so near to in the B minor symphony.

effect is shown by his having employed it again; first in the first repetition of the theme and then to an increased degree in the coda. But at least there are no grounds for the assumption that this was the source of his thematic inspiration.

Here an entirely different creative imagination was evidently at work. Let us glance for a moment at the harmonic progression of the first movement—at the change from B flat major to G flat major right in the *Hauptsatz*, the alternation between F sharp minor and A major in the *Seitensatz* of the exposition, and in addition the parallel sections of the recapitulation and the D minor of the development section playing into F major. Then in the *scherzo* (the *andante* with its broad harmony is a case apart) the alteration of the dominant in the fifth bar leading to the parallel key, and in the trio the hovering between B flat minor and D flat major. In short, the juxtaposition, contrast, and intermixture of parallel major keys and keys a third apart stands out as the characteristic stylistic idiosyncrasy of this sonata. And in the finale where the first episode deviates to G minor and the second theme contrasts F major and D major, our main theme in question is certainly in an atmosphere entirely congenial to it.

The conclusion to be drawn is self-evident. Neither the principle of tonal unity nor the idea of a modulation serving as organic connection link (as with Beethoven) characterizes Schubert's theme, but that imaginative urge to indulge in the interplay of the harmonic colors of changing moods, to mirror the delicate swing of divergent emotions in the magic of iridescent color which dominates the entire B flat major sonata.

"To the classicists, harmonic variation was an intellectual event; to the romanticists, a device for evoking moods, for enchanting the senses." If we now go by this dictum of Max Graf (8), then the Schubert of the B flat major sonata is a romanticist. And for that reason it is basically immaterial whether or no his theme was inspired by a recollection of the Beethoven theme. If this was really the case, then he failed to grasp the Beethoven theme in the sense of Beethoven logic. He heard in it, rather, the characteristic feature corresponding to his own imaginative tendencies (at all events in the conception of the B flat major sonata)—the harmonic play of color, the seeming tonal ambiguity. And Schubert's theme also sounds different to us as regards harmonic content. Here the outstanding feature is not the connection, but the alternation, between two keys. This is no theoretical sophistry. It is the "evidence of the ear" which hears in terms of broad associations and judges what is heard by the context. But from the context, the beginning of the Schubert theme (whose G at the decisive points reverts at times to B flat major or G minor) can also be understood in the "minor" sense, as interchangeable parallel of B flat major.

From this stylistic comparison of the two B flat major themes, we therefore carry away the nevertheless remarkable moral that the same "harmonic facts" can be taken at one time as a criterion of the classical style and at another as a characteristic of a "romantic" manner of writing.

CHAPTER IV

The Finale of the C Major Quartet

A study in form

As already pointed out in the first essay, Beethoven's Grand Fugue, in its fantastically intrepid architecture, represents a grandiose and unusually ingenious synthesis of fugue and sonata form. It would be rewarding to trace methodically for once the road that led to the conception of this unique creation; in other words, to study systematically the multifarious forms which testify to Beethoven's constant preoccupation with the problem of combining sonata and fugue form.

As stimulus and contribution to such an investigation let us analyze a Beethoven work written fully two decades earlier, which, from the aspect of the aforesaid problem, forms a counterpiece to the Grand Fugue: the finale of the third Rasumowsky quartet, Op. 59 (C major). This movement, which is often erroneously styled a fugue (2, 32) incorporates the same idea (i.e., the synthesis of fugue and sonata form) as the gigantic work of Beethoven's late period, even though in another style and expressive medium, and a different manipulation of the elements of form. By "synthesis" we understand a form which, in contrast to other combinations of the sonata and fugue principles, rests on a perfect mixture and inter-fusion[1] of the two compositional modes of thought.

For a better understanding of this, let us first of all examine once more the plan of the Grand Fugue, limiting ourselves briefly to those factors that are essential for a thorough understanding of the form. The ground plan corresponds to the structural form of a sonata, consisting of exposition, development, and recapitulation (along with introduction and coda). Two sharply contrasting double fugues, developed from two different variants of the theme, form the first principal section after the "pro-grammatic" *overtura* (which states the theme with its variants).

The first (*allegro*) in the principal key of B flat major, broad and dramatic in treatment, represents the *Hauptsatz* in the sense of a sonata exposition. The second (*meno mosso e moderato*) in G flat major, more concise in dis-position, represents, with its new counterpoint, the lyri-cal *Seitensatz*. The following section, opening and closing with the analogous parts of the marchlike *allegro molto e con brio* combines—and here lies the key to understanding of the form—the development technique of sonata and fugue; i.e., besides another rhythmically altered version of the theme, "motifs" (that is, fragments of the theme, which is broken up as in a sonata) are now worked out fugally. After such a thorough treatment of the theme, a recapitulation such as we would expect in a sonata move-ment is unnecessary. However, in the interest of clarity

---

[1] For fugue form, like sonata form, is more than mere "form." It is also more than a structural principle. Both, in the last analysis, are simply the essence of the actual musical logic of a definite epoch.

as regards the movement plan, it is not entirely suppressed but is indicated aphoristically. Before the coda, for instance, we find two bars of each of the double fugues (like quotations) similar to the two contrasting themes in the recapitulation of the sonata movement, both quotations in the principal key![2]

If we now turn to the finale of the C major quartet, our aim is merely to clarify the form and not to furnish an exhaustive description or aesthetic evaluation of the composition. We can hereby dispense with musical notations under the assumption that the reader has the score before him.

The movement begins like a fugue. In the interchange of dux and comes, three parts enter one after the other (viola, second violin, cello). Since the theme modulates to the dominant, the return modulation falls to the comes, which is effected by the usual device of deviating from the fifth to the fourth. But the entry of the third part already manifests a divergence from the norm of the fugue exposition; that is, the original version of the dux is not strictly maintained, but undergoes a change in the penultimate (ninth) bar, which leads to a tonic, instead of a dominant, close. And at the entry of the fourth part (first violin) which follows immediately, we find the dux again, contrary to the rules. The further development of the movement will show the reason for this ostensible anomaly.

First of all another feature strikes us about this independent "fugue exposition" and that is the lack of any consistent contrapuntal treatment, which from the very

---

[2] These quotations, which confirm our interpretation of the form, also have an entirely different significance than the outwardly similar "reminiscence motif" in the finale of the Ninth symphony.

outset is contrary to the assumption that Beethoven ever intended to write a real fugue. The "contrast" that answers the theme each time[3] and at first continues the theme's eighth-note motion and then changes to quarter notes, naturally has a very marked rhythm. But even at the first counterpoint, the quarter-note motif group (limited to chordal notes) leads to two bars of mere harmonic transcription (dominant seventh chord). At the next entry of the theme, two voices with the same rhythmic motion are counterpointed, the eighth-note figures of which (doubled sixths and thirds)[4] converge in quarter-note chords. And after the entry of the fourth voice of the quartet (first violin) the potentially four-part movement becomes two-part, doubled in octaves, in which the theme is allocated to the upper voices, the counterpoint to the lower.

The polyphonic texture ends temporarily with the compression to two parts. The last dux carried out verbatim for only seven bars progresses freely by means of a motif derived from the beginning of the theme—and destined for independent development later—which over a later equally important bass rhythm in half notes leads to the cadence in the tonic key. The pure homophonic section that this introduces modulates to the dominant of the dominant through a motif group of its own derived from the foregoing. And now a new idea appears in the key of the dominant[5] prepared by a connecting solo passage of the first violin—a short motif which is again des-

[3] Not strict counterpoint, to be exact; only the rhythmical configuration has been retained but not the melodic outline.

[4] Doubled thirds and sixths in a contrapuntal part as a Beethoven intensification device. See the trio of the E minor quartet and the trio of the *Ninth symphony*.

[5] In order to prevent any misunderstanding, the theme in G major begins on the dominant, that is, it is only apparently in D.

tined for polyphonic treatment carried out by means of repetition, limitation, and exchange of parts in double counterpoint (the eleventh) in periodic symmetry and expanded through elaboration of the motifs to a sort of binary song form with a cadential and again homophonic close.

In surveying the development of the movement up to this point, we recognize the ground plan of a sonata exposition. The presumable fugue exposition forms the *Hauptsatz*, the second contrapuntal section, the *Seitensatz*, while in between lies the usual modulatory part in homophonic texture. Now we understand why the *Hauptsatz*, contrary to all the rules of fugue exposition, states the theme twice in succession in the form of the dux. Here the object is to strengthen the principal key and to save the key of the dominant for the *Seitensatz*.[6] And the entry of a homophonic element into the fugue texture proves to be a special stylistic finesse, or more correctly speaking, the effect of a wonderful sense of homogeneous form, so that even the parts are imbued with the underlying idea of the work as a whole: the fusion of two different form types.

What the structure of the movement up to this point has revealed to us regarding the form is—to state the matter straightway—confirmed by a recapitulation which, *mutatis mutandis*, exactly corresponds to the exposition and in the fugal *Hauptsatz* even repeats the order of entry of the voices and the variants of the theme.[7] Bee-

[6] If we remember that Beethoven likes to introduce the modulatory part of his sonata movements with a (curtailed) repetition of the principal theme, the last (only seven bars) entry of the theme can also be interpreted in this sense.

[7] The only slight divergence is that the last dux retains eight instead of seven bars of its primordial form.

thoven's usual method of intensification in a recapitulation is achieved here by means of a new contrast," which is associated with the fugue theme from its very first entry and with its sharply profiled outline in half notes (only varying in unimportant details) plays the role of an independent and striking countersubject. Thus the quasi fugue of the beginning is now completed and even surpassed by a quasi double fugue!

We have skipped about 120 bars lying between the exposition[8] and the recapitulation: the development section, which proceeds directly from the exposition without any noticeable separation, in fact with not even so much as a double bar as a visible dividing line. It lies beyond the scope of our task to go into this part more closely, interesting as it is. The sole purpose of this study is to show that it is really a "development section" in the sonata-form sense, in which the fugue-form main theme is never once stated in its entirety,[9] much less undergoing a fugue-form "development." The contrapuntal technique, as an important device of Beethoven's art of development, naturally requires due space even here—and here especially—without interfering in any way with the brilliant unfoldment of other thematic elaboration.

A word still remains to be said on the coda, which corresponds with the development section not only in length (there are even more bars) but through the parallel form of the beginning (wherever one may assume the begin-

[8] It cannot be definitely decided where the development section begins, since the motivic chain work and the metrical motion extend beyond the usual tonal limits of the exposition and only reach a connecting point of repose in the realm of a new key (dominant of E flat major). The same is true of the transition from the recapitulation to the coda.

[9] The material of the modulatory section is taken into consideration, but not the *Seitensatz*.

37

ning to be).[10] Yet so far from unusual as such proportions are with Beethoven, just so little is this "parallelism" an isolated case (see, for example, the first movement of the Waldstein sonata). And furthermore, the last 105 bars (out of a total of 135 or 124) bear so unmistakably the character of a coda, even that of a *stretto*, that there can be no doubt about the form.

From all this it is difficult to understand how musicologists in general, and Beethoven specialists in particular, can consider this a fugue. It is far more justifiable to speak of a "sonata movement with fugal treatment." But this does not characterize the essential element of this form, namely, the fusion of the sonatalike and the fuguelike to a new structural form, which is identical with neither the one nor the other. For here the fugue parts do not represent inlays in the sonata texture, nor (as so often in Beethoven development sections) are they a result and product of thematic elaboration. They appear rather as structural carriers of the sonata idea, subject to the law of the sonata (as shown above) and in turn affecting the organism of the sonata (contrapuntal *Seitensatz!*).

[10] See footnote 8.

CHAPTER V

The "Problem" of the D Minor Sonata
(OP. 31, NO. 2)

Essay on a new interpretation of the form

IN the *Beethoven Handbook* (6, II, p. 203) Theodore Frimmel ridicules the investigations to which the peculiar form of the first movement of the D minor sonata has given rise.

It is really quite immaterial [he writes] what one calls the opening of this sonata, whether Introduction—though certainly not an introduction in the sense of those of the older symphonies—*Hauptsatz*, or "head" motif. At all events the first movement up to bar 21 remains *capriccio*like in character. If one chooses to have the *Hauptsatz* begin at bar 21, let him do so. I shall not interfere with him. Nevertheless this *Hauptsatz* rising within the intervals of the triad, takes form in the very first bar of the sonata so that it is merely a matter of taste if one places his H.S. [*Hauptsatz*] over the first or the 21st bar.

The sarcasm would be justified if the comments to which Frimmel refers were really only intent on applying the usual technical designations to the different sections

39

of the work, or (which amounts to the same thing) on fitting the movement to an ordinary schema. But something more important is involved. That is, to discover the underlying structural "idea" of a form that departs so strikingly from the ordinary principles. If for Frimmel, the historian, "the whole organic structure is sufficiently transparent," the musical theorists, who could not be content with such a purely intuitive understanding, have hitherto tried in vain to explain the law of this structure.

"The first movement of the D minor sonata [wrote Arnold Schmitz (37)] is extremely difficult to analyze. Even the question of where the first theme begins and ends brings up a ticklish problem." In his analysis of Beethoven's pianoforte sonatas, Riemann (32, II, p. 376, 379) also speaks of a "problem" (which Marx correctly recognized) presented by the very first theme of the first movement. He then goes on to confess that even his own analysis of form "by no means solves all the riddles." And when Nagel, the author of the other great monograph on Beethoven's pianoforte sonatas (26, II, p. 20 ff) attributes the "oddity of the form" of the first movement of this sonata to its "peculiar content" and attempts to solve a "series of enigmas" inherent in the form, from the psychological angle, he is merely shifting the argument, with its pressing questions, to another plane of observation.

Now in view of Beethoven's wonderful firmness of purpose in shaping his creative vision, the assumption is justified that the form of a Beethoven work will be "problematical" only so long as one fails to recognize, or misunderstands, the structural principle. Which fully justifies a new endeavor to fathom the much-discussed "problem" of the first movement of this sonata in order to discover the principle underlying this independent form;

that is, to find a point of view wherein the "anomalies" remarked hitherto appear as the logical effect of a homogeneous structural principle.

Since the movement, in the total layout in sonata form, does not begin with a principal theme of ordinary structure but with the contraposition of two sharply contrasting motifs underlined by a change in tempo, which are to undergo a broader development later, at the first glance one obviously takes the opening *largo–allegro* part (along with its intensified repetition) for an introduction and assumes that the actual exposition starts at bar 21. Here, at the return of the tonic, a new *allegro* melody begins, which is developed from the *largo* motif and in so far as its shaping and its inner content are concerned, might well be taken for a "principal theme."

But this interpretation, which is also held by Leichtentritt (19), proves to be untenable. It is chiefly invalidated by the fact that the presumably principal theme does not reappear in the recapitulation. The absence of the principal theme in the recapitulation would be just as incompatible with the sense of the "recapitulation" as with the idea of the "principal theme" according to the classical concept. For the "resumption" of the thematic idea of the exposition is not based on considerations of symmetry alone. Its real, structural significance rests rather on the changed relationship between the thematic parts which—apart from the influence of the development —is the result of assimilating the tonality of material whic' was first introduced in contrasting keys. And in this ' cess of unification to the principal tonality, how co' original representative of the tonic key, the ' theme, ever be omitted? If it should be wanti' development section, it would also lose i' principal theme; taken in connection with the whole, it would appear only as a point of departure, not as a developmental factor.

For this very reason the part in question (from bar 21) cannot be the principal theme.[1] Furthermore it also lacks one decisive characteristic of a principal theme. The principal theme of a Beethoven sonata movement regularly represents and circumscribes the principal key, no matter how extensive the scope of the tonality may be. But in this case it is a question of a pattern, the development of which leads in thematic elaboration from the principal key to the dominant of the dominant, that is, of a section having the typical structure of the usual transition from the first to the second theme.

Naturally Riemann and Nagel already recognized this fact, but they both disregarded it in favor of preconceived points of view. For Riemann the part in question remained the "real germ of the first theme," which resulted in his constructing a "first theme" that includes not only this "thematic core" but also the two previous *largo-allegro* sections.[2] But Nagel, with the antitheses "purely formal" and "in reality," tried to get round the contradiction by sensing the modulatory part as "actual *Hauptsatz*" and

[1] Leichtentritt assumes that the principal theme has been "skipped" in the recapitulation "since it has been very thoroughly treated in the development section and if it were repeated again in the recapitulation it would lose its impressiveness." That means either that Beethoven is guilty of a structural error or that one supposes a treatment of form appropriate to the romantic mode of thinking but not to Beethoven's structural and compositional methods.

[2] This contributes nothing towards a real understanding of the structure. Just why the "real core of the first theme" should be missing in the recapitulation remains an open question, as does also the question (which will be discussed later) how the motivic material for the second theme ever got into the ambit of the first theme.

"increased effect of the thematic core." And yet in spite of all he has to call it a transition.

Schmitz (37) was the first to draw the only correct conclusion from the fact that the transition begins at bar 21. "Therefore the theme must have really been stated in the preceding bars."

But on going into the matter further ("but where, that is the question") he too arrives at a *non liquet*. "If the question is presented from the traditional angle, then in this movement of sonata Op. 31, No. 2, it remains a picture puzzle as it were." For the section in which we should expect to find the "first theme" [bars 1–20] "presents no real thematic complex, not even a complex thematic core, but merely individual components which are separated one from the other by various tempo indications (*largo-allegro*) and by *fermatas*." Therefore "the only thing, finally, that can be called a theme here (bars 1–20) . . . is merely an attempt at a theme, an improvisation."

Is this argument of Schmitz's really convincing? Strictly speaking, it is based only on the change in tempo and the *fermatas;* for "the contraposition of two fundamentally different motifs, or motif groups, is an old property of well-written instrumental music." (4) Now it is impossible to see why Schmitz, in marked distinction to the "tension *fermata*" in bar 6 of the E flat major sonata, Op. 31, No. 3, defines the *fermata* on the last note of the *largo* of the D minor sonata as "separating." That here we also really have to do with "tension *fermatas*" can be seen from the harmonic treatment. The first *largo* is in th' dominant harmony, followed by the *allegro* in the to' even though it returns subsequently to the dominan' is the most elementary harmonic "tension relati' according to current ideas (and *mutatis mutan'*

43

ly in the second *largo–allegro*), and the *fermatas* only tend to increase the "dominant tension." The first *largo–allegro* (with prolonged *adagio* close) forms a perfect unity. That there is also a metrical unity was already brought out by Riemann (leaning on old Marx) when he wrote: "If the note values for the *largo* are taken at exactly double the value of those in the *allegro*, then the symmetry is in fact perfect." Finally, as regards content, the *largo* and the *allegro* complement each other in the sense of "theme and antithesis," "statement and contradiction," or the like; and the impression of the close relationship of the contrasting structural links is confirmed and heightened still more through the correspondence between the first and second *largo–allegro* parts. (To be conscious of this, just imagine that bars 7 to 20 have been deleted.) Therefore if the beginning of the movement alone were in question, the only really unusual factor (as Blessinger (4) also pointed out)[3] would be the change in tempo, which heightens the contrast.

The "problem" of the first movement of the D minor sonata becomes very much simpler the moment we see that the complex of the first six bars (in spite of the two-tempi structure, which is misleading at first glance) may well be a "theme." For as soon as we recognize the first statement of the *largo–allegro* as theme, we find a com-

---

[3] "The way Beethoven forms the theme in this case was in itself quite usual in the classical period. . . . The only peculiarity in this Beethoven thematic treatment lies in the fact that here the distinct contrast is heightened still more through the contraposition of two diametrically opposite tempi." Nevertheless Blessinger also cannot seem to bring himself to recognize the first largo–allegro simply as "theme." For, after quoting the first four bars, he continues: "A second period gradually develops from this introduction, which is directly connected with it and is outwardly more homogeneous." (Here he quotes bars 21–24.)

pletely normal layout of the recapitulation. First of all it begins with the same "theme" as the exposition, which is then followed by the C major repetition of the *largo* (by dispensing with the second *allegro* answer). The theme thereby undergoes an intensification through the recitative growing out of the *largo,* as always happens with the themes in Beethoven's recapitulations one way or another. As far as form is concerned, this recitative and its pendant after the second *largo* are naturally no longer puzzling, since Riemann (32, p. 383) recognized it as a constituent part embedded between the original members of the theme. After this partly expanded, partly curtailed, but unmistakable repetition of the *Hauptsatz* (as we may now call this part) the recapitulation does not perchance "skip" a substantial part of the exposition but, in keeping with the exposition, brings a "transition" leading to the *Seitensatz.* Since this part has to fulfil a different function in the third section of the sonata form than in the first (connecting two parts of a movement that are of identical rather than contrasting tonality), in the recapitulation it differs regularly from the exposition. However much we may marvel at an inventive power which here gives the recurrent "transition" an entirely new character, there is essentially nothing strange about this deviation from the corresponding portion of the exposition. Even a casual glance will show us that in other respects the recapitulation then progresses in a thoroughly analogous manner. So it need only be mentioned for the sake of completeness.

This would prove first of all that no part of the movement ever breaks through the logic of the sonata idea even deviates from the usual movement plan of the s form. But this proof—conclusive as it may seem— first be taken only as hypothetical. For up to no suance of Schmitz's point of view, we have only found that the *largo-allegro* takes the place of a principal theme and viewed by itself can really be a "theme," as far as structure is concerned. But a further question, and perhaps the most important and interesting one connected with this theme, has never even been touched upon in the foregoing examination. The fact that one experimented so long with the concepts "device," "introduction," "improvisation," in order to grasp the sense of this *largo-allegro*, and that neither Riemann nor Nagel, Leichtentritt nor Schmitz arrived at such a seemingly obvious and, in our opinion, practicable solution of the form, cannot be due alone to the varying tempo indications. To come right down to it, the really problematical factor is not the configuration of this "theme" in itself, but its relationship to the movement as a whole. "To begin with, the first motif is really the principal motif of the movement so that the leading eighth-note figure of the *allegro* is determinative for the *Seitensatz*." With these words Nagel tried to lay bare the essential. To be more exact, the most remarkable thing about the initial theme is that its second component contains the germ of the *Seitensatz*.

The section that follows the "transition" like a "second theme"—which we must view as the thematic core of the *Seitensatz* (bars 42–55)—unmistakably derives its motivic characteristics (the upbeat eighth-note movement with feminine ending as well as tonal repetitions so characteristic of the melody) from the first *allegro*. Therefore even Marx (22, 1, p. 143) recognized that the *Seitensatz* had its origin "in the *allegro* entering after the first and second *largos*." And the recent investigations of Eugen Schmitz have, in the same sense, led to the conclusion that the group of bars in question "is not original, but derivative."

However, when in the face of this Blessinger (4, p. 189) like Riemann before him, recognizes only an "unchanging eighth-note figuration," the mere listing of such obvious similarities still seems insufficient to elucidate satisfactorily the sort of relationship with which we have to do in this instance. Therefore, if our analysis is to rest on a firm foundation, we must not fail to prove our claim regarding the origin of bars 42–55.

Unclarity or doubt with respect to the given relationship can only be due to the fact that the primordial form of the motif introduced in the first *allegro* does not reappear in the second theme. But does it not undergo a metamorphosis right after the second *largo?* No one will deny that these bars (8 ff) represent an intensified resumption and further continuation of the first *allegro*. Furthermore, a sketch cited by Nottebohm (30, p. 27)—which has the second *allegro* begin as an exact transposition of the first —confirms this analogy. If we now consider the nature of the change that takes place in the motif of the first *allegro* in the process of the harmonic and metrical expansion to the second *largo*, we then recognize that the deviation from the primordial form rests on augmentation and change of direction of the interval steps, whereby the note repetitions, which result originally from suspensions, now appear partly in the form of auxiliary notes and anticipations.

EXAMPLE 18

But the same principle of the motivic development that operates in the second *allegro* (in itself "the most usual

47

transformation of a motif because the least menacing as regards its recognition") (33, I, p. 9) leads logically from the motivic configuration of the second *allegro* to the motivic figures from which the "great period" of the second theme is formed. It is only necessary to compare the opening bars of the two passages to convince oneself of this.

EXAMPLE 19

Thus the main portion of the *Seitensatz* is the result of a gradually progressive developmental process which extends not only to the motivic material itself but also to the metrical units formed therefrom (and increasing from step to step at that).

We must now learn to grasp the underlying sense of this peculiar structure. The first assumption is that the movement plan incorporates a structural idea of earlier days. Does not the motivic origin of the beginning of the *Seitensatz* remind one of the pre- and early-classical sonata form in which the first and second themes derive from a common root? As a matter of fact Beethoven returned to this structural idea on several occasions (in his pianoforte sonatas, in the first movement of Op. 2, No. 1, Op. 57, and probably Op. 49, No. 2). Very true, the sense of his form here is diametrically opposed to the corresponding structural idea of the older masters. For Beethoven proceeds—at least this is true of the *Appassionata*[4]—from

---

[4] Even though Beethoven, as Riezler (35) brings out, added the second A flat major theme later only when the work was already well under way.

48

the principle of two contrasting themes for which those precursors were striving as yet. The type of movement in question from the early period of the "classical sonata form" is directly characteristic of the change in style which the two-theme principle (current later on) achieved only gradually as against the still popular idea of the "unity of the theme."

Such considerations raise a question that in turn resolves for us the structural idea of the first movement of the D minor sonata. Can the aforesaid portion of the *Seitensatz*, which is nothing but a new developmental stage of the first *allegro* idea, lay any claim whatever to the designation of a "second theme" such as Riemann and Bekker as well as Schmitz and Blessinger unhesitatingly accord it? If a Philipp Emmanuel Bach or a Haydn develops from the motivic material of the principal theme a theme expressly destined for the *Seitensatz*, then this refashioning of the material is apparently intended to provide a contrasting idea to the first theme, or at least something new, something different. But in Beethoven's D minor sonata there can be no question of such a relationship between the *Seitensatz* and the initial theme. Here the *Seitensatz* does not proceed from a transformation of thematic material for the sake of contrast, but from the further development of a thematic idea which in its original version is already effective as a contrasting principle. In this case the purpose of the *Seitensatz* is not to introduce a new factor of contrast but to carry out an already existing one. How could its themelike core—however much it may resemble a theme—be considered a new, second "theme" when it lacks not only motivic independence, but also the property of contrasting with the theme from which it develops?

49

But from another point of view also—that of the harmony—it would not be permissible to identify the pseudo second theme as a real "second theme." While the real second theme of the classical sonata exposition is in the contrasting key, the presumable second theme in the first movement of the D minor sonata represents merely a fragment thereof—a gigantic dominant that awaits tonal completion. True, its last note brings it just within the range of the tonic, but how could this one quarter note, which is already the beginning of a new motivic section, be of any importance in the face of a fourteen-bar organ point that rivets the whole complex into the harmonic unity of a dominant?[5] And especially, since this dominant component of the key of the *Seitensatz* proceeds directly and unnoticeably from the modulatory section in such a way that the harmony attained from the main key, as dominant of the dominant, changes into a dominant of the contrasting key without intervention of the new tonic.

The mighty dominant block at the entry of the *Seitensatz* postulates a correspondingly broad establishment of the tonic; the tremendous piling up of the harmony demands a broad expansion of the tonality. But this supplement, which is harmonically and metrically necessary and rounds out the key, is effected with new material.[6]

For this reason we could not simply call the motivic unified section (the special subject of our examination) a

[5] In a seemingly related case (the second theme of the first movement of the F minor sonata of Op. 2) the situation is really entirely different, since here the organ point already clears the way for a cadence in the first period.

[6] In this final motif (*a–b♭–a–g♯–a*) many claim to recognize the motif with which the upper voice answers the largo motif of the bass in the modulatory section (bars 22–23). The question need not be gone into here since it is of no importance in our investigation and cannot be decided definitely one way or the other.

Seitensatz. We had to resort rather to more specialized designations. One will not do justice to this peculiar structure by trying to apply to it schematically the ordinary technical terminology.[7]

The second part of the exposition (calculated from the beginning of the organ point, bar 41) shows, it is true, two sections of different motivic material; but the harmonic progression disregards this structure (*Gliederung*). The second complex beginning with the tonic of A minor (bar 55)—thematically a unity of inseparable, interlocking, motivic members riveted together and growing one out of the other—is, as cadence, indissolubly connected with the first, the "pseudo second theme." It could be taken for an "epilogue" if, before its entry, a second theme were present, or if the *Seitensatz* were already completed as a unified whole, in the tonality sense. But the tonality of a *Seitensatz* only results from the union of the "pseudo closing group" and the "pseudo second theme." Therefore the sections *Seitensatz* and "closing group" are fused here into an inseparable unity.

The statement that the second part of the exposition contains no theme of its own, that the principal thematic idea of the *Seitensatz* plays neither the role of a contrasting "second" theme nor evidences in any way the formulation of a "theme," provides a definite answer to the earlier question as to the relationship existing between the antithesis *"largo-allegro"* and the movement as a whole. This answer, which removes every vestige of the "problematical," and lets the structural idea of the movement come out clearly and completely, can only be: the

[7] This is also true of the attempts of Riemann and Nagel to subdivide it, with contradictory results.

antithesis *largo–allegro* at the beginning of the movement is really "theme" and not (as it might seem before examining the *Seitensatz*) a questionable "first" theme, one half of which might belong to the *Hauptsatz* and the other half to the *Seitensatz*. But it is *the* theme pure and simple, the *only* theme of the entire movement.

In this one theme, the contrast, which we otherwise usually find in the relationship between the two themes, is anticipated *in nuce*. Therefore in accordance with the logic and economy of Beethoven's structural methods, it is neither necessary nor possible to introduce a second theme. The idea behind the further progress of the exposition is to develop the theme according to its individual nature, that is, to "intensify" the contrast presented at the beginning, to carry out the dualism of the theme. Beginning with a simple contraposing of the contrasting motifs within the narrow space of a six-bar theme, the "battle of two principles," which is the underlying idea of this highly dramatic composition, constantly increases in intensity and scope. In this respect the *Seitensatz* bears the same relationship to the "modulatory section" as the first and second *allegro* to the first and second *largo*. In the development section (note the triple statement of the *largo* motif), this thoroughgoing intensification principle reaches a climax (with the result that the conflict, which has been pressing for a decision, is finally decided: after the last onrush of the *"largo* motif," the presence of the *"allegro* motif" is only still revealed in the undulation of its accompanying figures). We have already spoken of the thoroughly regular treatment of the recapitulation as compared with the exposition.

According to a much quoted and commented statement by Czerny,[8] Beethoven while at work on Sonata

Op. 31 is supposed to have said that he "wanted to take a new path." If our interpretation of the form is convincing, then Beethoven's structural idea for the first movement of the D minor sonata is far more novel and simple, more daring and logical at the same time, than all the former analyses led one to suppose.

[8] Quoted from (16, 1, p. 46). Thayer's version (40, 11, p. 362) is slightly different.

CHAPTER VI

Two Comments on the A Flat Major Sonata, Op. 110

I

The running passage in the first movement

IN the first movement of Beethoven's A flat major sonata (Op. 110) the transition from the *Hauptsatz* to the *Seitensatz* takes the form of a running passage in sixteenth notes, which represents a series of chord figurations employing an independent motif which is neither evolved from the *Hauptsatz* nor introduced in the *Seitensatz* and which only approximates to the motif of the new theme (octave leaps) just before the entry of the *Seitensatz*.

Although this finely-etched and musically-melodious figure work, which represents the ornamental accompaniment of the first section of the recurrent principal theme at the beginning of the recapitulation, forms such a characteristic component of the exposition that it can lay claim to a place not only in the parallel passage of the recapitulation but also in the coda, it still seems that as far as substance is concerned we must consider it a purely figurative interpolation between the actual "thematic" parts.[1] And this gives rise to the question how an apparently un-

---

[1] Cited by Leichtentritt (19) as a transition with running passages.

related running passage in a late Beethoven work achieves structural independence as the carrying idea of the transition and how the figurative element comes to operate as an organic component of the composition and to give the effect of being artistically homogeneous—as an expressive medium—with the rest of the material.

It was really Marx (22, ii, p. 254) who first raised the question when he called the sixteenth-note passage "very striking . . . and contrary to Beethoven's methods, by no means motivated by what had gone before."[2] And Wilhelm von Lenz (21, v, p. 71–72) seems to have sensed the presence of something hidden behind the "seductively charming" figured passages ("zephyrs in the acanthus and the ivy of the portico") even though the clue that he chanced upon in studying the coda was also of doubtful value and led nowhere. "Short appendage in the tonality of Part I [he writes]. Hidden beneath these aeolian harp tones, as under leaves and blossoms, is the original question represented by the notes c, d^b, b^b (bass, eighth and following bars before the close)." But if one consults the two special works on Beethoven's pianoforte sonatas by Riemann (32, iii) and Nagel (26, ii) it will be found that even modern literature offers no clarification of the question.

Riemann is merely voicing an emotional reaction when he says (p. 423) that "the passage work of this entire movement is such an important constituent of the thematic invention that it never for a moment gives the impression of a virtuoso effect." For he offers no criterion that would define the sixteenth-note figure as "thematic." Instead, he goes on to say (in contradiction to his previous

---

[2] The words omitted from the above quotation are not entirely clear.

comment) that "even the sixteenth-note arpeggios of the appendage of Periods I, V,[3] and VII are nothing but a harmless embellishment, a light mist that conceals the momentary stagnation of the development section and from which the outlines of new melodic forms emerge again all the more charmingly." If the word "harmless" is meant to banish again the suspicion of a "virtuoso nature" in the sense of outward effect,[4] the word "ornament" and even more so the above-quoted metaphor of the "light mist from which the outlines of new melodic forms emerge all the more charmingly" nevertheless characterizes the running passages in question as embellishment in contrast to the thematic material of the work!

But in speaking of a "momentary stagnation of the development section" Riemann again contradicts his findings in the form analysis a few pages earlier (p. 420) in which he assigns the role of an "evolution section for modulating to the key of the second theme" to the appendages of Period I (i.e., that part of the exposition in sixteenth notes). But Riemann's use of the term "evolution" still expressly stresses the fact that "development" is the real task and nature of that section of the movement that is to effect the entry of the contrasting key and a contrasting theme.

Nagel (26, p. 346) views the "arpeggios" as a "running passage," the "rhythmic precision and energy of which prepares a new phase of the movement, which comes out more and more in the transition to the second theme." That is, in his opinion the "transition" only begins at bar 20 where (as Riemann recognized) the second

[3] This should be VI. V is a typographical error in the Riemann text.

[4] "To use such passages for virtuoso effect is equivalent to slapping the composer in the face" (p. 424).

theme actually begins (26, p. 347; 32, p. 420). While Nagel expressly denies, even though only parenthetically, "any serious possibility of there being any relationship between this passage and the preceding part," he states that "first of all the music-making found in this figure is that already characterized so often as unpremeditated ... a free play of fantasy in which an idea traverses vast spaces of the tonal realm as though lost in dreams." He seeks the threads of a logical connection in the progression of the bass: "the characteristic motif of the bass (bars 13–14) and its further progression" is to him the "factor" that "recurs immediately, as always in such cases in Beethoven's music" and "frees the ideas from the domination of capricious fancy."

So long as there was no clear understanding of the formal disposition of the movement, as quotations taken at random from older works reveal directly or indirectly,[5] it was difficult to view the sixteenth-note section other than as episodic passage work, which one had to accept—

[5] Marx (22, p. 254) touches on the question of form only indirectly in the above-quoted reference to a part writing "contrary to Beethoven's methods." But he gives himself away by selecting just this passage (odd though it seems to him compositionally) (bar 12 ff) as the point of departure for a poetic interpretation of the movement: "In the Ossianian sense it is the farewell from the beloved harp. Once more the weary fingers wander over the strings . . ." [The sixteenth-note passages certainly give little evidence of "weary fingers"! Moreover, see the beginning of "Mitteilung Herrn Prof. Schindler's an Uns," quoted by Lenz (21, p. 112).]

Lenz (p. 71–72) presents a structural plan that is not entirely comprehensible in spite of the numbered bars, in which the *Seitensatz* ("contrast" in the dominant) seems to be assumed from bar 28 (as with Nagel), although bar 34 is characterized as "counter motif" ("more a flattering tonal figure than a *cantilena*.") According to Wasielewski (48), "Beethoven again approximates more closely to the sonata form in the two first movements of Op. 110." "If the opening movement, quite apart from its often dreamy, gentle character, has some-

57

with or without any attempt at motivation—as an anomaly in style and form. Nagel still holds this point of view.

Through an erroneous designation of the second theme, he has so distorted the form that he is now unable to find a place for the sixteenth-note section in the regular structural scheme of the sonata. And since he can adduce no organic reason for it, his explanation can be nothing more than a makeshift. For Riemann, on the other hand, knowledge of the form was a fundamental prerequisite to an explanation of the presumed anomaly. But, as we have shown, he failed to carry his investigation to its logical conclusion.

Once we admit that bars 12–19 form the transition from the *Hauptsatz* to the *Seitensatz*, we arrive at the following:[6] In a number of his sonata movements, Beethoven

thing fantasy-like about it, the development-like use of the two initial bars in the middle portion of the same, and also the following repetition of the first section, is reminiscent of a sonata movement." To Deiters (40, IV, 235) the movement—which he also misjudges in another sense—is reminiscent of the "old sonata form." He says among other things that "here it never comes to a really clear-cut second theme." Bekker (3) is also influenced by Deiters in his characterization of the movement, though more with reference to content than to form.

[6] What stood so long in the way of a proper understanding of the structure is obviously the harmony. Even Riemann (who recognized the transition in retrospect from the second theme) says that the second theme, which he identified "according to the transposed reproduction," begins "with (8 = 1) in which, since A flat is still the tonic, the 8 = 1 brings the harmonic equivalent T = S" (*sic!*) (25, p. 420). This is beside the point. On the contrary, from bar 16 on, the modulation moves so definitely towards E flat major that the harmony with which the new theme begins in bar 20 can only be heard as subdominant of the new key and that, inversely, an A flat major full cadence should have to follow in order to make the beginning of bar 20 (retrospectively) credible as the tonic of A flat major! Riezler (35) analyzes in the same sense the harmonic progression through which "the entry of the second theme is curiously disguised, for it opens, immediately after the sixteenth-note arpeggios, in what sounds like A flat major but is really the subdominant of E flat. Only by degrees, after the series of trills in the bass, is the E flat clearly asserted."

lets the transition grow directly out of an already initiated and more or less intensified repetition of the principal theme by fusing the repeated portion of the principal theme and the following modulation into one uninterrupted section.[7] If we visualize this structural process, then in seeking some relationship between the transition and the principal theme in the first movement of the A flat major sonata, we will not overlook the fact that the first four bars of the transition correspond to the harmonic progression after the first four bars of the movement—the "head motif," as Riemann calls this essential idea, or core, of the main theme[8]—i.e., the chord series of bars 12–15 is composed of the principal harmonies (chords at the beginning of the bars) of bars 1–4:

Bars 1 and 12 tonic;

Bars 2 and 13 dominant, passing four-three chord;

[7] Examples: first movements of the pianoforte sonatas Op. 31, No. 1; Op. 53; Op. 57; Fourth and Seventh symphonies; *Egmont* overture (borderline and transition cases apart). Mozart employs the same procedure in the first movement of the great G minor symphony.

[8] The whole *cantilena* up to the beginning of bar 12 is to be understood of course as the "main theme." The relationship of the "head motif" (which is really a motif complex, forephrase of a virtual period) to the following thematic section will be clear when one recognizes, first of all, that the rhythm of the melody from bar 5 on is a variant of bars 1–2, and further when one notes that the bass line of bars 5–8 is a variant of the bass fundament of bar 1 up to the first beat of bar 3 (extension of the dominant bass from bar 2 over two bars), and last of all when one takes into consideration the analogy of the melodic factors bars 3–4 and 10–11 which correspond to a half and full close. While Lenz (21), who treats the two sections of the theme as question and answer, already seems to have recognized that the second has grown out of the first as the "more developed melodic idea" (p. 71), the concept "introduction" or "curtain," which Riemann suggests for the first four bars of the "head motif," or "theme head" (p. 419–20), leads to the assumption that he has overlooked the relation of the second section of the theme to the first, as brought out here.

Bars 3 and 14 tonic, sixth chord;
Bars 4 and 15 dominant.

The fact that the dominant in bar 4 (expanded to the dominant seventh chord on the second quarter note) does not return to the root position in bar 15 but to the six-five chord does not affect the agreement, but is premised by the different architectonic mission of the two analogous bars. The object of bar 4 with the *fermata* is a strong caesura, wherein the "head motif" is contrasted with the following; bar 15, on the other hand, a further development without caesura.

EXAMPLE 20

At first there still seems to be no tangible basis for this statement; for in spite of the striking similarity of the bass progression, the analogy after all consists only in a symmetrical interchange of tonic and dominant.

But from the beginning of the recapitulation, a clear, new light falls on the relationship of the two passages. Here where the figures of the transition play round the "head motif" in the manner of "ornamental variations," it is revealed that bars 12–15 (the rest is a logical continuation of the content of these bars) represent the ornamental form allotted to it (and actually added in the recapitulation).[9]

[9] The connection will come out more clearly if the three passages are envisaged in a different order: (a) the "head motif" as it appears at the beginning of the movement; (b) the "head motif" with its ornamental sheath as it appears in the recapitulation; and (c) the ornamental sheath without the thematic core, as presented in bars 12–15 (beginning of the transition).

The beginning of the recapitulation, which at first glance seems to confirm the purely figurative character of the transition, shows in point of fact that the tendrils of these running passages have sprung from thematic soil. This explains the logical and organic effect inherent in the seemingly free play of the sixteenth-note arabesques. The transition really goes back to the beginning of the principal theme, but it merely indicates the thematic idea (to which it has reference) between the lines, so to speak. It presents the harmonic ground plan of the primordial theme by means of a new motif (variation motif). Instead of the actual corporeality, it brings merely the fragrance, as it were, of the theme in question.[10]

Here we have an example of the "veiled texture" which Riezler cites as a criterion of Beethoven's last style.[11] But—leaving aside the irrational in the creative process—it was an artistic-economic motive that impelled Beethoven to let the "head motif" in the transition appear only "latent" behind the veil of a newly introduced figuration: he did not wish to weaken the effect of the wonderful *cantilena* through prolonging repetition, but to enhance it by contrast. And so the running passage, which

[10] An analogous case, which *mutatis mutandis* is traceable to the same technical device, is found in the first half of the Fourth variation (Tempo I) in the *adagio* of the E flat major quartet, Op. 127. Here for the space of four bars the only reference to the theme is found in the tempo, the meter, the main points of the harmonic progression and a few turns of the new and seemingly freely invented melody of the first violin. With the upbeat of the fifth bar, however, the theme which was only "latent" heretofore is now actually present in the cello part, while the first violin takes up the former line of the cello part (trill motif and ascending triplet figure) and identifies it as *obbligato* accompaniment to the theme (for the entire variation), and real varying principle (*Variierungsprinzip*) of this variation.

[11] "It is just the transparent, almost immaterial texture, and the delicacy of contour and tenderness of expression that is most truly representative of his last style" (35, p. 255).

was added with the unaffected ease of "unpremeditated music-making" and developed to an "important constituent" of this inward tone poem was inspired by the same "great wisdom" which, according to Riezler (35, p. 231) induced "Beethoven to refrain from allowing the song theme to appear again in the recapitulation."

II

The harmony in the trio of the second movement
In discussing the second movement of Beethoven's A flat major sonata, Op. 110, Nagel (26, p. 354) touches upon the harmony of the D flat major middle section as follows: "The principal key is that of the lower major third of the tonic; the second sections modulate to G flat major and its parallel minor." Then he goes on: "It is impossible to state definitely how the harmony of the section is to be understood in detail since the bass steps do not offer a sufficient clue."

Musical theory would be a sorry matter indeed if it were unable to define the harmonic processes in this "trio," as this section of the movement should be briefly designated. The analysis of another writer, to which Nagel himself alludes in a footnote, also contradicts his *non liquet*. "Riemann [32, p. 431] makes a very ingenious attempt at analysis." This raises the question why Nagel did not adopt Riemann's analysis instead of claiming that it was impossible to analyze the harmony in detail.

Riemann (p. 432) also finds that the single notes in the left hand indicate the harmony "only very imperfectly." But no more "imperfectly," one can interpose, than is inherent in the nature of two-part writing! However, he aptly points out that these single notes suggest that a change of harmony takes place only every four bars; that is (as he illustrates in musical notation), four bars tonic, bars five to seven dominant, and the eighth tonic again.

If Riemann had retained this sensible aural interpretation as the basis of his theoretical analysis, the difficulties of his task would have been limited to the classification of the melodic elements proper and foreign to the harmony. "But [he said, thus contradicting his own admittedly "suggested" interpretation] that is hardly correct." Instead of this, the following illustration from his *"Skizze der Analyze,"*[12] with its functional letters, shows how he really understands the harmonic progressions.

EXAMPLE 21

If one seeks the grounds for such an interpretation of the harmonic relations, one can only look to Riemann's analysis of the melody at the very beginning of his exposition of the trio (p. 431–32). He says, namely, that "the player can only be safeguarded from a serious mistake by whittling out the melodic core from the eighth-note figuration." For the "harmonic notes (chordal notes) are transcribed in part with the upper and lower auxiliary notes, and in part, not." Riemann illustrates his assumed distribution of auxiliary notes and notes proper to the harmony by the first four bars of the melody in which functional letters indicate which notes in the bracketed

[12] The question of phrasing which the graph, with its arbitrary grouping of the notes, brings up at the same time is not taken into consideration here.

eighth-note groups he understands each time as "notes proper to the harmony."

EXAMPLE 22

Then, over and above this, the entire forephrase of the first period of the trio is traced back to the version given below, with the statement: The actual melody is as follows:

EXAMPLE 23

Naturally this is no more the "actual melody" than the wonderfully animated and inspired melodic line is a figuration[13] or even an epitome (according to Riemann's interpretation) of the notes proper to the harmony, but a figure crystallized from the melody by a purely subjective method.

After this glance at Riemann's harmonic analysis, it is quite understandable that Nagel's musical instinct re-

[13] This is true at any rate when one, like Riemann himself, has in mind the antithesis between "figuration" and "melody," and does not confuse this clear, necessary, and customary differentiation with antitheses perhaps of another kind, such as "absolute" and "figured melody," "chordal motif," and "figuration motif" (see 4, p. 114, 164). Moreover, to characterize the trio melody of Op. 110 as "eighth-note figuration" is on a line with Riemann's claim (33, I, p. 20) that "on closer inspection the presumably logical continuation of one and the same motif in the first movement of Beethoven's C minor symphony turns out to be only the maintenance of a definite form of figuration."

fused to recognize this. How can the b^b in bar 2, which accords with the a^b of the bass, be taken in a subdominant sense, especially since the alteration of the subdominant root follows immediately after in the melody? How can the a^b over the bass f in bar 3 be taken for a factor of the dominant seventh chord? And what is the basis for assuming that the g^b in bar 5 (which is without proper harmonic support) represents the subdominant? Since the ear still hears the a^b of the bass from the preceding bar at the entry of the g^b of the upper voice, and the bass leaps to the dominant third c, a b^b should actually have to be intercalated between these two bass notes if the g^b of the melody were to be understood as subdominant root instead of dominant seventh.

Granted: Riemann's functional indications would represent an acceptable harmonic analysis if the upper voice alone were in question. That is, Beethoven's melody could be harmonized as Riemann hears it if the original accompaniment (and the tempo proper to it!) were unknown. But Beethoven has "harmonized" it differently.[14] And herein lies the fundamental error of the Riemann interpretation: it is based on a one-sided consideration of the upper voice.[15]

[14] It goes without saying that Beethoven never "harmonized" anything as though he first invented the melody and then added the harmony. Naturally the invention of the melody without the harmony appertaining to it is unthinkable and the inherent harmony of the melody, from the very first moment on, was also not altered artificially (which would be quite conceivable).

[15] That Riemann himself was far from convinced of the soundness of his harmonic analysis is shown by the fact that he demands "that the sub-dominants indicated in the upper voice must be brought out in spite of the seemingly contradictory harmonic indications of the left hand." He cannot overlook the fact that the bass contradicts his interpretation, even though he tries to get round it with the help of the adverb "seemingly."

If we hear the melody as it should be heard, in conjunction with the accompaniment that fills out the harmony, the harmony comes out clearly and distinctly and the interpretation that Riemann finds obvious by virtue of the lower voice, but rejects in view of the deliberately isolated upper voice, turns out to be the conclusive and only possible one for the musical ear. The bass notes of the first four bars thus represent the factors of the arpeggiated tonic triad. The manner of the figuration makes it possible to hear a twice-broken five-three chord, or the root position followed by the sixth chord.

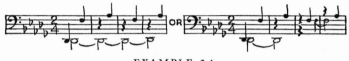

EXAMPLE 24

And the bass *c* of bar 5 confirms the *g*♭ of the upper voice as dominant seventh[16] and thus binds bars 5–7 to the harmonic unity of the dominant.

The following musical notation, in which the melody is traced to its proper harmonic components, lays bare the harmonic framework of the first eight bars of the trio.

EXAMPLE 25

[16] We can only speak of confirming the *interpretation* of the dominant seventh, because at the entry of the *g*♭, as shown above, the previous *a*♭ of the bass is still in the ear and is now interpreted as the dominant root.

So far for the judgment of the unbiased ear. It is not the result of, but the prerequisite to, theoretical considerations and therefore precedes the detailed analysis which we will now undertake.

The first bar requires no elucidation. But to offer a completely satisfactory theoretical explanation, we must investigate bar 2 all the more thoroughly. The first eighth note (the a^b of the melody which enters without accompaniment) in following immediately on the preceding (with the tonic harmony still in the ear!) can only be understood as the tonic fifth. Since a change of harmony within the bar is not expected at this rapid pace, the ear is naturally inclined to apply the initial harmony of the bar to its entire content. The ear is influenced here first of all by the musical "probability."[17] For whether or no the bass note a^b, which falls with the dissonant b^b of the melody,[18] is to be taken as the carrier of the tonic or the dominant harmony, can be decided only at the resolution of the dissonant chord, which no longer occurs within this bar.[19]

[17] "The probability of the progression of the parts is decisive for the interpretation," etc. (17, p. 199. See also p. 194, par. 2, line 12 ff).

[18] It goes without saying that the quarter note in the bass, sustained below the eighth-note motion of the upper voice, is the harmonic carrier and the b^b of the melody represents the dissonant component of the chord. The fact is only mentioned here in view of Riemann's contrary opinion.

[19] The following shows that the nature of the harmony is only definitely determined by the progression of the parts. If the upper voice should return from b^b to c at the fourth eighth note, then the bass note, and with it the whole bar, would be dominant (considered as upbeat phrase from the second eighth note and the entire bar in the sense of a downbeat phrase, by subsequent alteration of the function of the first eighth note). If the fourth eighth note were a^b, then the bar might sound dominant, but it could also be taken for tonic. If the upper voice jumped from b^b to f instead of g (as it actually does in the third bar), there would be no doubt about the tonic function of the bar. This double interpretation can naturally arise only in the

The fourth eighth note of the upper voice, the altered auxiliary note *g* (which delays the resolution beyond the bar) points, it is true, to its own tendency note *a♭* as resolution note of the dissonant *b♭*, but it does not yet reveal whether this *a♭* to be expected in the upper voice will appear in the quality of the tonic fifth or the dominant root. The next bar brings the solution. After a suspensionlike return to the dissonant *b♭* and the insertion of an *f*, the upper voice brings the resolution note *a♭* over an *f* in the bass, which has been resting up to this point. The bass note of the second bar therefore stands between fragments of the tonic chord (without being filled out harmonically to the dominant).[20] It is confirmed as a factor of the tonic harmony. The melodic note *b♭*, however, is shown to be the tonic sixth, which enters the harmony in the form of an auxiliary note. It relieves the tonic fifth only temporarily[21]

EXAMPLE 26

and besides, only in the upper voice while the bass completes the arpeggiation of the tonic triad.[22]

theoretical analysis. The ear grasps and evaluates the harmony, not in its momentary aspect, but at once as member of a more extensive concatenation.

[20] The *f*, inserted as second eighth note between the *b♭* and the *a♭* in bar 3 is also a fragment of the tonic triad, which would be sufficient to fix the tonic harmony as *sound* (as sixth of the previous bass note *a♭*) but not rhythmically (unaccented note).

[21] See (17, p. 75) regarding use of tonic sixth as simple passing note.

Tonic Triad

EXAMPLE 27

Nevertheless, the sixth carries so much of the color of the tonic "substitute" (parallel tonic, VI degree) into the harmonic unity of the principal tonic chord that it seems well to take this harmonic effect into consideration subsequently in the sketch of the harmonic progression, after a melodic process is found to be the determining cause.

EXAMPLE 28

The suspension effect of the repeated note b^b in bar 3 rests on the thereby indicated replacement of the real tonic harmony by a "deceptive chord," which in a four-part harmony would look like this:

[22] Fritz Roegely in his *Harmonie Lehre* (p. 159) interprets similarly the tonic sixth over the long sustained C major triad in the first movement (bars 4–5) of the Schubert string quartet. ("A is not a sixth but only an expanded fifth.")

EXAMPLE 29

The eighth note *c*, which precedes the *b*♭, is naturally an auxiliary note, and was also so designated by Riemann. The succession of three auxiliary notes in bar 2 offers no difficulty theoretically. *B*♭ and *g* circumscribe the harmonic note *a*♭ and only *c* is an auxiliary note of an auxiliary note.[23] Moreover, the auxiliary note *b*♭ (if it seems more convenient to look at it in this way) can be called the "principal note" in the aforementioned sense (a substitute harmonic factor, or more exactly, an added sixth).

The following graph, in which the *c* is notated as an appoggiatura and the notes *b*♭ and *g* as a bichord, may illustrate the relationship of the auxiliary notes to each other and to the real harmonic components of this passage.

EXAMPLE 30

Here the double stems on the note in the upper staff show that also in this interpretation of the theoretical facts of the case, the "artificial leading note" *g* leads to *a*♭, the next chordal note but one, and not to the adjacent note *f*, which

[23] Regarding such cases, see (17, p. 210).

departs only momentarily from the direction set by the
g.[24]

Since the melodic note a^b in bar 3 is a tonic fifth, the
following fourth eighth note g^b (still over the bass note f!)
naturally cannot have the function of a dominant seventh.
It is really a passing note leading to the f of the fourth bar

EXAMPLE 31

which through the interpolation of the auxiliary note e^b
plays itself the role of a passing note

EXAMPLE 32

and as such is repeated after the e^b

final

EXAMPLE 33

[24] It seems well to mention this here since Brahms uses the similarly altered auxiliary note, in a downward direction, in the *a cappella*
movement *In stiller Nacht*, bars 8–9. But here (see 17, p. 261) there are
good reasons for it, as otherwise we would have parallel fifths.

Since Riemann also did not question the tonic nature of the fourth bar, the situation is so clear that any further elucidation is superfluous.

We have already explained why the first eighth note of the fifth bar cannot be taken as the subdominant, but only as dominant seventh. The harmonic unity of the dominant, which extends to, and through, bar 7, begins at bar 5. It is unnecessary to analyze bars 5–8 individually. The following graph, in which the notes foreign to the harmony, in the form of chords or grace notes, are differentiated from the material proper to the harmony, may serve to amplify the foregoing. Therefore in each bar the upper voice contains two notes proper to the harmony, with the exception of bar 2, in which however, the auxiliary note b^b, following the chordal note a^b, may be considered a "substitute" harmonic component.

EXAMPLE 34

It was not the inherent difficulty of the material itself that necessitated such a minute investigation of a group of eight bars, as the results of the analysis show. Rather, it was prompted by the necessity of refuting an erroneous presentation of the musical facts and of solving an extraneous problem. Any still outstanding details in the harmonic analysis can be settled in a few words.

The afterphrase, which rounds out the first eight bars

to a period (bars 9–16) repeats the four opening bars of the forephrase, then to begin the modulation with an extension of the tonic (bar 13), which is achieved by what Klatte (14) calls "dominantization" of the tonic; that is, a new interpretation and expansion of the tonic triad to a dominant seventh chord of the subdominant key G flat major (bars 14-15). Here the entirely different effect of bar 13, as compared with the melodically identical bar 9, deserves notice. Coming right after the melodic step *f–d♭* over the bass note *a♭*, the *f–c*, no longer supported by the bass note *d♭*, has a special color lightly suggestive of the III degree.

The forephrase of the following G flat major period (bars 17–24) is a transposition of bars 1–8. The modulation to the parallel key of E flat minor, which falls to the afterphrase (bars 25–32), takes place over the parallel dominant.

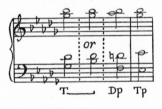

EXAMPLE 35

The parallel dominant, which occupies one bar in the above graph, extends over three bars (29–31) in the composition, since the E flat minor sound (*Klang*) that results at the second quarter note in bar 30 is a "deceptive chord," without functional independence. Even though formed by a *nota cambiata* (*Fuk-sche Wechseltöne*) (*e♭* and *g♭*) it could be taken at most for a "passing" tonic triad, since it rests on the passing harmony

EXAMPLE 36

transformed through the melodic progression to

EXAMPLE 37

The single expansion of the two-part writing through the three-note chord in bar 29 is not so much for the purpose of clarifying the chord in itself (which one of the two bass notes would also make sufficiently clear) as for indicating more clearly the progression of the parts.

EXAMPLE 38

At the same time this deviation from the existing compositional pattern represents an almost imperceptibly fine means of intensifying the sound (*klangliche Steigerung*) up to the two chords effecting the return modulation to the main key. And from this point of view an exception that is apparently necessary only *ad hoc* is shown to be a measure systematically calculated to the "whole."

To obviate such misunderstandings as Riemann's construction of the "actual" melody, it is perhaps not out of place to recall at the close of this exclusively harmonic analysis that our dissection of the melody is not intended to—nor can it—teach anything regarding the structure of the melody as such. Citing the notes proper to the harmony only contributes to an understanding of the harmony, but it does not give us the "melodic core" in the sense of the concentrated melodic substance. Merely to seek such a "melodic core," in contradistinction to a "figuration," is to mistake the nature of this melody. (See footnote 13.) The thematic analysis finds the germ cell of the melody in the tenderly eloquent double motif[25] which, independent of the momentary harmonic significance of the individual notes, or group of notes, is purely melodic in substance.

EXAMPLE 39

[25] The melodic development departs from the regular progression of the double motif in only two passages in the entire trio: the chords of bars 34–35, which go back to the double octave leap of the phrase connection in bars 8–9 (and its imitations at the group). The simple, clear layout, however, does not prevent Nagel from speaking of the trio as "perhaps the strangest of all Beethoven forms," since he so grossly mistakes the character of the work as to find in it "the typically Beethoven obstinacy'" and "his delight in uncouth boisterousness." Has Nagel perhaps so misunderstood the *sforzati* at the beginning and at the melodic caesuras, which manifestly have to do with the pedal effects? (The text in question in the Breitkopf & Härtel *Urtext* edition is really a little confusing and should be gone over again carefully. Naturally too hasty a pace (and Nagel himself warned against this) can distort the picture by destroying the *cantabile* quality of this very pronounced *piano* melody, which should be viewed as a lyrical contrast to the explosive F minor *Hauptsatz*. True, it is a *cantabile* quality of a very special kind, inherent in the even flow of the notes of small value, and Riezler (35, p. 230) is quite right when he stresses the fact that the *allegro molto*, "particularly in the expressive figures of the melodic section," belongs to Beethoven's "last style."

CHAPTER VII

The Thematic Treatment of the Egmont Overture

Refutation of a wrong interpretation and false conclusions

(To the manes of my friends Dr. Erich Loe-wenthal and Theodor Liedtke who lost their lives in Ausschwitz—and who loved this over-ture)

I

IN his work *Das Romantische Beethovenbild* (p. 156) Arnold Schmitz says with reference to E. T. A. Hoffmann's interpretation of the *Egmont* overture that "anyone who wishes to adjudicate the true character of the overture must naturally first have a clear picture of the thematic and motivic structure. In other respects Hoffmann makes some clear-sighted observations on thematic and motivic associations, but here he overlooks important factors. That in the introduction and the *allegro* up to the coda all the motivic treatment develops from the two main motifs

EXAMPLE 40

and is dominated by their contrast was brought out by
Riemann and Heuss in their analyses."

As a matter of fact Hoffmann, in his essay on the
Egmont music, was guilty of several inconceivable over-
sights. For example, so far as the overture in particular is
concerned, he failed to note that the closing *allegro con
brio* is nothing other than the anticipation—prolonged by
a six-bar introduction—of the Victory Symphony, less its
own two opening bars.

But Schmitz did not have this in mind in his remarks
quoted above. He regrets, rather, that Hoffmann, who
naturally did not fail to see how important the first motif
(Ex. 40-a) of the *sostenuto* is for the *Seitensatz* and the
coda of the *allegro*, did not notice the connection between
the main theme of the *allegro* and the second motif (Ex.
40-b) of the *sostenuto* claimed by Riemann and Heuss. In
Hoffman's opinion, namely, the main theme of the Allegro
(or more exactly the preparation of this theme) does not
enter until bar 15. (He himself says "in fact.")

If the following examination sets out to show that, in
the sense of Schmitz's criticism, Hoffman did not overlook anything, but Riemann and Heuss saw too much, it
is naturally not a question of justifying Hoffman—in itself of no importance. The point is rather the clear perception of a Beethoven movement plan, which is distorted by the interpretation of Riemann and Heuss. The
refutation of this erroneous interpretation, however, seems
all the more imperative since under the authority of the
three names, Riemann, Heuss, and Schmitz, an error
threatens to achieve the value of an "established verdict."

That the *Seitensatz* and coda of the main movement
(*allegro*) of the *Egmont* overture in the structural form

of a sonata are rooted in the first motif complex of the introduction (bars 2-5) can be taken as "evident." The development of the main theme of the *allegro* from the motif introduced by the first violin in bar 15 of the *sostenuto* is equally unequivocal. However, a relationship between the main theme of the *allegro*—or also its germ motif developed from the fifteenth bar of the *sostenuto* on—and the second motif of the *sostenuto* (bars 5-8) is *not* evident. On the contrary, if the claim is made, it must first be proved or brought out in analysis. And with this proof stands and falls Riemann's thesis (40, III, p. 240-41) that the "contrast—stated right in the opening bars—between the Spanish autocrat characterized by the broad Sarabande rhythm (Ex. 40-a) and the enslaved Dutch raising their hands in supplication (Ex. 40-b) dominates the entire overture."

Now on what does Riemann base his thesis? He first declares summarily: "The two motifs of the *allegro* are only transformations effected by diminution," and he then proceeds to cite several musical examples (among which are the first four bars of the main theme of the *allegro*) with the accompanying comment that "they derive from 'b' through preparation, in fact before the entry of the *allegro*," which he illustrates by quoting the germ motif from bar 15. But he does not touch on the decisive question of what the descending violoncello melody, which is the core of the main theme and the germ motif from which it springs, have to do with the motif of the opening bars 5-8.[1]!

[1] Since in his quotation of the main theme of the *allegro*, Riemann, at the second quarter note of the third bar, jumps from the line of the violoncello part to the here overarching melodic phrase of the first violin (*c–f–e*) and cites as a further motif ostensibly arising "from Ex. 40-b" the figure of the first violin from bars 18–19 of the *allegro*

But Heuss (9) in his work has repaired Riemann's omissions. He tried to bridge over the cleft between motif 'b' (as the motif in Ex. 40-b is briefly characterized) and the germ motif of the main theme of the *allegro*, which appears in bar 15. The second entry of motif 'b' (bars 12–13 of the introduction) furnishes him the connecting link. The melodic line, which is here allocated to the clarinet (Ex. 41-c) is, in his opinion, a version of motif 'b,' whose "womb already contains" the motif from bar 15 of the introduction. To make this clear he cites the motif from bar 15 in augmentation, transferred to the metrical unit of the "object of comparison."

At first glance this comparison is very intriguing:

EXAMPLE 41

It presents two phrases in approximately the same meter, differing only in the time of entry and the value of the last note. Both contain the descending melody b^b–a^b–g^b–f and move in the direction of the final note f as main center of gravity. However, on closer examination it will be found that the assumed resemblance is an illusion.

We need not go into the question of how far the motif

(f–f–e–e, etc.), one might assume that he attributes the significance of a "motif" to the descending semitone beginning with the upbeat (which can naturally also be found in 'b'). In the light of Riemann's examples, it is not at all clear what he really understands by "the two motifs of the *allegro*." But the third example quoted in the same connection, the figure of the first violin, which "bursts in victoriously" in bars 50–51, contradicts the aforementioned assumption. Nevertheless, we will find the same interpretation by Heuss, who holds that the semitone step indicates a relationship between the second motif of the introduction and the main theme of the *allegro*.

in bar 15 retains its real meter in the meter assigned to it in the augmentation as shown in Ex. 41-d.[2] For also in this version of the motif, which is assimilated as closely as possible to Ex. 41-c, the distribution of the strong and weak beats in the melodic line b^b–a^b–g^b–f is entirely different to that in the example. The accents inherent in the "fractional beats"[3] are so distributed that the top note b^b and the g^b (in Ex. 41-c) fall on a weak beat while the exact contrary is true in Ex. 41-d. (The double accents indicate the centers of gravity of the bars.)

EXAMPLE 42

The agreement of the melodic notes gives the phrase a visible resemblance at most, but never an aural one, i.e. for the musical perception. But, furthermore, motif 'b' occurs nowhere in the clang of the overture in the configuration shown in Ex. 41-c, which Heuss views as transition form to the motif in bar 15! And in the notated score also, this motif configuration is only to be found— a picture puzzle as it were—when the melodic fragment of

[2] If the augmentation is to reproduce the upbeat motif exactly as it appears in bar 15, then at all events the initial note a^b must remain an upbeat, that is, the bar line must come after this note. (Whether the following bar line then belongs before or after the last note is a question of interpretation, since the motif in itself could be interpreted in common or in triple time. Or it depends on whether the augmentation is to be written in two- or three-part time). At all events Beethoven himself proceeded differently with the augmentation of his motif in the last bar of the introduction. He placed the four descending notes on the second and third beats of the bar, thus providing the model for Ex. 42-d, but with the decisive difference that the upbeat is retained, by not participating in the augmentation.

[3] "*Spaltwerten*"—Riemann's terminology.

the first clarinet given in Ex. 41-c is viewed quite by itself, divorced from its continuation and without considering the accompanying parts. According to the actual sound and the motivic sense, Ex. 41-c, starting with the major-mode version of motif 'b,' is not a motif unit but a fragment of a more extensive motivic chainwork; and just that descending melody (*b*♭–*a*♭–*g*♭–*f*) which for Heuss was apparently the *tertium comparationis*, is cut, through the demarcation of the motif, into two divergent sections; namely, pieces allocated to different motivic units. We will first offer indirect proof of this.

If the melodic fragment of the first clarinet were heard as it appears in Ex. 41-c (that is, in Heuss's version), then the following entry of the first flute would bear a symmetrical relationship to this phrase:

EXAMPLE 43

The melodic leap from the final note *f* of the first phrase to the first note (*e*♭) of the second would thereby form a dead interval. But since the upper voice—which the ear follows—passes without a break from the first clarinet to the first flute (thanks to the part writing and instrumentation, which will be taken up later) the leap of the seventh (*f*–*e*♭) strikes one as a highly characteristic melodic movement; and this seventh will be recognized as the unmistakable hallmark of motif 'b,' even as the seventh (*c*–*b*♭) of the clarinet, which immediately precedes it. In view of the pregnant form of motif 'b,' no further explanation is required. If one recognizes the first four notes of the melody, beginning at bar 12, as the major-mode version of motif 'b,' one will also recognize the four following notes as the fourth transposition of this motif. And although this time the motif is allocated another position in the bar than at its first entry in the minor mode, it maintains its own rhythmic accentuation and determines the structure of the melody accordingly.

Motif b   Motif b

EXAMPLE 44

This logical structure, however, is (as already shown) perfectly natural for the ear through the part writing and instrumentation. For while the first statement of motif 'b' in the major mode is allocated to the solo voice of a clarinet in a deceptive *stretto* with a bassoon, the fourth transposition of the same motif in five-part writing for wind instruments is so carried out that in "real" four-part writing the melody sounds in octave doubling. This really demarcates the motif clearly enough!

The transfer of the melody from the first clarinet to the first flute, which takes place in the middle of the motif, and the simultaneous diversion of still other parts[4] necessitated by it, produces, it is true, what at first glance seems to be a somewhat complicated score, the misunderstanding of which might well have been the point of departure of Heuss's wrong analysis. But the reason and purpose of this instrumentation is easy enough to grasp. The three-

[4] The first clarinet instead of the second assumes the further octave doubling of the melody while the second clarinet continues an inner voice temporarily begun by the oboe.

lined *b♭* of the clarinet would not be mellow enough to continue the melodic line in the desired timbre. On the other hand, the corresponding register in the flute, mixed with the deeper octave of the clarinet, produces the quality demanded by the intended expression; at the same time it is so similar to the previous tone color of the two clarinets progressing in octaves that the uniformity of timbre is assured. Following this necessary exchange of the flute for the highest register of the clarinet, the other exchanges in the parts take the easiest, simplest course (that is, diversion to an adjacent voice). The solo voice of the assisting oboe (which does not play an independent role, as sixth voice, until two bars later) also proves to be a logical way of filling out a clear aural picture. In short, what here might seem misleading for the eye is ingeniously right for the ear.

Although Heuss's whole motivic sorites collapses through the now demonstrated untenability of his decisive premise (i.e., the motivic relationship which he claimed to find in Ex. 42-c and 42-d) we have still to examine one point that he brings forward in support of his contention.

He tries to establish a direct, albeit loose connection between the primordial form of motif 'b' and the main theme of the *allegro* by asserting that the first three notes (*c–d♭–c*) of the main theme of the *allegro* hark back to the "semitone cries of pain," which he characterizes as "elements" of motif-complex 'b.'

True, it is only a question of intimations: calling motif complex 'b' the "theme of suffering" and the main theme of the *allegro* the "theme of strength and suffering"; slurring on the first three notes in the graph of the main theme of the *allegro* to correspond with the semitone steps taken from motif-complex 'b'; and through the linkage with the thematic-poetic interpretation of the overture. The word "motif" is never used, and it is not altogether clear whether the semitone is to be understood solely in the interpretative sense[5] or as motif. But from either viewpoint the tonal connections under comparison (i.e., motif 'b' and the main theme of the *allegro*) have nothing in common with each other but the diatonic semitone. In motif 'b' (which Heuss divides into two semitone steps) and in its imitations,[6] a note proper to the harmony forms the center of gravity of the descending semitone in upbeat rhythm. At the beginning of the main theme of the *allegro*, it ascends and descends a semitone to and from a sharply dissonant note foreign to the harmony (auxiliary note) as center of gravity of the bar.[7] Furthermore, the fact that in the major mode, which we find at the opening of the main theme in the development section, this semitone step has been changed to a whole tone,[8] shows how very unimportant it is as a hallmark of the motif.

[5] (Trans. note.) The author employs the term "hermeneutic sense" here, which in English properly applies only to the interpretation of the Scriptures. Hermann Kretzschmar (leaning perhaps on Schleiermacher) introduced it into German aesthetics about 1900 as a designation for his method of "interpreting musical motifs as the expression of human emotions." This method, which was also adopted by other writers (Heuss, Schering) is similar to the *Affektenlehre* of the eighteenth century, but is unknown in English aesthetics and musicology.

[6] Although the descending semitone in upbeat rhythm at the beginning of motif 'b' is so characteristic that it suffices to represent the motif at the imitation, Heuss's division of the motif into two semitone steps, in which he ignores both the "tension of the seventh" and also the actual meter, must seem nonsensical.

[7] It is not necessary here to go into the variants of the original forms—the syncopic prolongation of the upbeat in the viola part (unison with the first bassoon) in bar 8 and the metrical shifting of the semitone $d\flat$–c in the further course of the main theme of the *allegro*.

From the previous examination we find that the roots of the main theme of the *allegro* do not go back to motif 'b,' but really only to bar 15 of the introduction. That a change takes place in the developmental process at this bar, that here a new principle begins to operate, a new carrier of the action as it were, is not only brought out by the striking rhythmical contrast of the newly introduced motif itself,[9] but is still further underscored by a change of motion and color in the accompaniment, which might be compared to a change of scenery (vibrato of the second violins and violas in sixteenth notes and accentuation of the weak beats by sustained chords in the wind instruments). The introduction thus consists of two distinctly

---

[8] In the second edition of his book (9) Heuss shifted the center of gravity of his demonstration by slurring on semitone steps to all the pertinent graphs (eight in all) thus making a main argument of the semitone step. Since the notes db–c and gb–f have been slurred on in Ex. 42-c (our notation) but in Ex. 42-d only the semitone gb–f, the *tertium comparationis* of the descending melody (bb–ab–gb) falls into the background and attention is focussed on another accidental resemblance: that is, the beginning of Ex. 42-c with the semitone step db–c, which occurs three times in the first four bars of the main theme of the *allegro*, and is slurred on in the graph in question. Since no changes were made in the accompanying text, except for some small stylistic retouchings, the alteration in the graphs only confuses the issue—which requires no further refutation after what has been said above.

[9] The deliberate intention of this rhythmical contrast—underscoring the independence of the new motif— is shown very clearly by the fact that the motif is introduced in diminution (as *Unterteilungsmotiv*) and appears in its real shape only in the last bar of the introduction in note values corresponding not only to the principal meter of the introduction (as "bar motif") but manifesting approximately the same pace as in the *allegro* (imagined quarter note = quarter note). If, in comparison with the preceding form of the motif, and the only one known to the listener up to this point, the version of the motif in the last bar of the introduction appears to be "augmentation" (see note 2), the further course of the work shows it to be the permanent and normal form so that in retrospect the preceding version of it is identified as "diminution."

contrasting parts of thematically different content. The first part only furnishes the *allegro* with material for the *Seitensatz* and the coda, while the preparation of the main theme of the *allegro* is reserved for the second part of the introduction.

The contrast between motifs 'a' and 'b' developed in the first part of the *Sostenuto* (up to bar 15) is accordingly not meant to expand into a sonatalike contrast of the main and second themes or to "dominate the whole overture" in any other way. It can be considered only as announcement or basis of analogous contrasts that motif 'a' undergoes in the *allegro* within the *Seitensatz* and the coda. It is therefore impossible to decide conclusively whether or no the *piano dolce* phrase, which carries on a dialogue with motif 'a' in the second theme, is really derived—as Riemann contends—from motif 'b.'[10]

The only things that might point to a derivation from motif 'b' are at most the general direction of the intervallic steps (down-up-down) and the fusing together of the interlocking parts. But these are far-fetched rather than striking resemblances and are of no importance in comparison with the fundamental dissimilarities of the two figures.[11] For this reason it is obviously more to the point

[10] "In the second theme the two confront each other again in their original form ('a' and 'b')." Apart from the question raised above, this comment of Riemann's (32, p. 241) is inexact inasmuch as motif 'a' does not appear in the "original form" in the *Seitzensatz* by any manner of means, but in a variant thereof.

[11] One really striking resemblance, which calls for interpretation—though there is no proof of its having been intentional—is that between the motif in the second theme of the overture (which contrasts with motif 'a') and the reminiscence motif in interlude IV (*larghetto*, bars 1–4) derived from interlude II (bars 18–21 and 46–49). The closing motif from *Klärchens Tod* (the last eight bars) might also seem to be related. Bekker (3) considers these three motifs from the overture, the interludes, and *Klärchens Tod* to be identical.

to consider the "fleeting flattering addition" (as Marx (22) calls the motif connected with motif 'a' in the *Seitensatz*) as a new contrasting idea independent of motif 'b.' In addition, there is still a second contrast to motif 'a' at the close of the *Seitensatz*, and in the Coda there is still another

EXAMPLE 45

(which apparently reverts to the previous closing motif of the epilogue).

EXAMPLE 46

If the contrasts in the *allegro*, which could be related to the antitheses 'a-b' stated at the beginning of the overture, only denote contrasts within thematic units (i.e., contrasts of the second degree), then the contrast between the main and second themes of the *allegro* can be definitely and clearly traced back to the *sostenuto*, and what is more, in two ways. First by contrasting the part represented by the motif group 'a-b' with a section that prepares the main theme of the *allegro*—just as in the *allegro* a second theme (which lets motif 'a' alternate with a contrasting motif) is contrasted with the fully developed main theme; and by playing off, in the second part of the introduction, motif 'a' as bass against the germ motif of the main theme of the *allegro* unfolding in the upper voice.

II

If, in refuting the contentions of Riemann, Heuss, and Arnold Schmitz, we have succeeded in clearing up the real thematic treatment, we have attained the object of our investigation. But the examination of motivic inter-relationships that was necessary to this end carries it automatically beyond its original scope. It not only helps to give us an undistorted view of the structural layout of the work that we sought; at the same time it furnishes us new hints for understanding the compositional plan of the "formative idea" that is inherent in the objective structural process (*Gestaltung*).

In comparing the contrasts in the second theme and coda with the antithesis at the beginning of the overture, it must strike one at once that motifs 'a' and 'b' are co-ordinated only in their contrasting juxtaposition but not as regards their importance in the total movement plan of the work.

The role of motif 'b' is played out in the first part of the introduction with two entries—one complex developed from the version in the major mode and another from that in the minor. But even though motif 'b' should appear in the second theme, that is, if that portion of the theme alternating with motif 'a' were to be considered a transformation or derivation of motif 'b,' it would still remain episodic in character.

Motif 'a,' on the other hand, plays a leading role. It remains effective so long as the unity of the movement that it introduces is uninterrupted, namely, up to the transition to the Victory Symphony, which is independent thematically of the foregoing. It stands like a rock at the beginning of the whole, the herald of a tragedy to come.

As bass of the second part of the introduction, it accompanies and influences the first movements of the arising adversary (the formative main theme) like a menacing shadow in the background of the scene. As core of the *Seitensatz* it enters into the development with imperious energy, and in the coda has the last word as demonstration of a terrifying and, at the close, actually destructive power followed only—before the transition to the apotheosis of the Victory Symphony—by that exciting bar in which the violin motif is interpreted as the "sword thrust" which seals Egmont's fate.[12]

One striking characteristic of motif 'a'—apart from its basic dramatic encounter with the forerunner of the main theme in the second part of the *sostenuto*—is that we find it paired with a contrast each time it enters. These changing contrasts, which like trenchant secondary roles enrich, differentiate, and deepen the working out of the main idea and, from the dramatic point of view, are naturally auxiliaries of the antagonist of motif 'a,' serve particularly to heighten and supplement at the same time the effect of motif 'a' itself; through the contrast relationship they enhance its expressive power and lend it indirect dramatic activity by representing the momentary coun-

[12] (32, p. 241) and (3, p. 346). It is worth while to point out that this "sword thrust" is represented by the same motif that (as shown above) is taken over into the coda from the closing group where it confronts motif 'a'—timidly and pacifyingly— at first *piano*. If we are correct in interpreting the bar in question as the "sword thrust of the executioner"—and this is at least plausible—the motif with its changing interpretation would afford us an instructive example of how, under the influence of the "programmatic," the motifs and themes in Beethoven's music are also primarily and fundamentally figures of the musical fantasy which, as Unger puts it (43) are developed according to the rules peculiar to music and can only incidentally and by way of exception assume the significance of fixed symbols for extra-musical ideas (in the sense of modern program music or the *Leitmotif* technique of Richard Wagner).

tereffects engendered by its presence. In this sense the impressiveness and comparatively detailed structural shaping of its first contrast corresponds to the tremendous power of the tonal configuration in which motif 'a' is introduced. And this explains why the episodic character of the role played by motif 'b' could be misunderstood.

It goes without saying that motif 'a' finds the real goal of its dramatic activity in its relationship to the main theme. That the psychological cause of the dramatic argument between motif 'a' and the main theme lies with motif 'a' and that the role of "antagonist" is actually forced upon the main theme by motif 'a' cannot be more clearly shown with the resources of instrumental music than occurs in the introduction to the *Egmont* overture. After a tremendous expansion of motif 'a,' the main theme only develops gradually from a weak germ awaiting "augmentation,"[13] and this over a bass foundation traced out by motif 'a'! Motif 'a' thus proves to be a musical manifestation of a "tragic principle" which as "agent" opens, premises, intersects, and decides the symphonic "action."

Finally if one associates the "tragic principle" (21, IV, p. 207; 22, p. 135; 48, II, p. 76) with the idea of despotism, as personified in Alba—which is the traditional interpretation and finds its justification in the relationship between composition and poem—it can be understood why the motif, which forms the mighty corner pillars of the movement (exclusive naturally of the Victory Symphony), could not produce the main theme for the *allegro* but was allocated its place in the second theme within the actual sonata form. The tragedy to which Beethoven wrote his

---

[13] This interpretation is not in disagreement with the statements of footnote 9. It only brings out that there is a musical as well as a descriptive intention behind it.

overture is not entitled *Alba,* but *Egmont.* Thus the main theme, or *Hauptsatz*—in symbolizing the figure of the protagonist[14]—expresses the idea of tragic suffering and revolt. Furthermore, by leaving to the coda the full display of power of motif 'a,' it is an indirect characterization but clear description in music[15] of the tragedy of defeat.

The survey of the role of motif 'a,' even without programmatic interpretation, teaches us that its entry in the *sostenuto* cannot have the secondary structural importance of a "preparation" of the second theme of the *allegro.* As a rule, motivic material, which in the introduction or the transition section precedes the statement of the theme for which it is to furnish the material, serves as a preparation for the theme in question. But the tempo and note values (meter) alone give the *sostenuto* version of motif 'a' such superiority over the version in the second theme of the *allegro* that von Lenz (21), with his perceptive feeling for the existing relationship, could say that that the "quarter-notes in the contrasting motif of the

[14] Bekker expressed this pertinently and clearly (3, p. 245).

[15] Here one theme "silences" another literally and figuratively. As opposed to this "indirect" representation of a tragic end, the *Coriolanus* overture offers a "direct" one. There the theme "dies" like the hero in Collin's tragedy—right on the stage before the very eyes of the spectators, so to speak. But this does not mean that the close of the overture is an unequivocal description in music of the physical death of the hero. Nor can there be the slightest question of its depicting his suicide according to the situation in Collin's tragedy. The underlying thought of the final version of the theme is best expressed by the following quotation from Richard Wagner's programmatic interpretation: "But this obstinacy has now become the man's sole vital energy. Coriolanus, without his revenge, without his destructive rage, is no longer Coriolanus, and he must die if he relinquishes his obstinacy" (49). The rhythmical consistency relaxes, the theme grows quieter, breaks apart. See also (43).

allegro (bar 58 and following bars) are the diminutive of the heavy steps of the *sostenuto* in half-notes." Moreover, the figure that Schmitz (37) characterizes as the "main motif 'a' " is, to be more exact, more than a "motif."[16] In fact it is a motif group, which as a "result of the germinal force of a motif" would even fit Riemann's definition of a "theme," as given in his Dictionary (34). And a piece of "motivic elaboration" develops from this in the *sostenuto* and is continued in the *allegro* in the form of the second theme and the coda. But here it is of slight importance whether or no this theme corresponds structurally to the prevalent concept of the classic sonata theme.[17] It should only be understood as "theme" in a functional sense, in the abstract basic significance of the word as the "sentence" which expresses the ideas that are to be worked up.

[16] It is neither necessary nor, in view of the divergence of opinion as to what constitutes a motif, is it possible to demarcate motif 'a' exactly. It suffices to say that in no circumstances can it extend over more than two bars which comprise the combination of the downbeat and the upbeat motivic rhythm. In the writer's opinion the motif represents one bar with the rhythm: eighth note|half note, half note, quarter rest, eighth rest.

[17] According to Riemann's definition of the word "theme" in his Dictionary, "the themes of a sonata movement are the result of a long-spun-out development of a motif" (34). See also the differentiation that Riezler attempts to draw between theme and motif (28, p. 247). If only a larger complex is to be considered a theme in the sense of the sonata form, one is at liberty to take bars 2–9 as such. Since motif group 'a' modulates to the dominant and motif group 'b' back to the tonic, the two together form a tonally complete "eight-bar statement." The objection that the working out (except at the quasi repetition of the whole, which follows immediately) makes use only of motif 'a' is hardly sufficient to invalidate this interpretation. From the functional point of view, the influence of motif 'b' nevertheless continues as first example of the contrasting complement demanded each time by motif 'a.' All the subsequent arguments set forth above are also quite in keeping with the assumption of a theme extending from bar 2 to bar 9.

There is all the more reason for assuming this "primordial theme" (as we will call it to differentiate it from the main and the second themes of the actual sonata movement represented by the *allegro*) if the structural members developed from motif 'a' are considered from the standpoint of "thematic elaboration." The four-bar motif group, which stands like a rock at the beginning of the overture, is curtailed to a two-bar group (one-half of the primordial theme) at the quasi repetition of the antithesis 'a-b.' In one-bar form, namely in the upbeat rhythm without the antecedent downbeat,[18] the motif serves to represent the modulating bass line in the second part of the *sostenuto*, then to be broken up finally in the three last bars before the entry of the *allegro*, leaving only a rhythmical atom. In the *Seitensatz* of the *allegro*, the motif is tautened again to a two-bar group and expands once more to the original four-bar group in the coda.[19]

In structure, the coda with its three motif groups 'a,' each alternating with a contrast, corresponds to the second theme; extended to four-bar motif groups, it outdoes it. With the four-bar groups it re-establishes the broad line of the primordial theme; with the three-motif groups, it exceeds it. Thus we have a working out process which begins with the fragmentation of the primordial theme into ever smaller components, then by means of a synthesis carried out in two steps, to lead to the mightiest of

[18] The upbeat, which opens the bass version of motif 'a,' is authoritative proof that here only a single bar—cut off from the bulk of the motif group (the second)—furnishes the material for further treatment.

[19] The curtailing of the last motif group 'a' in the coda has naturally nothing to do with the technique of thematic or motivic division, but represents a highly dramatic disruption of the symmetry through the force of the catastrophe. The "sword thrust" falls in the fourth bar, in fact.

the figures (*Gestaltungen*) formed from motif 'a.' (The fundamental rhythm of motif 'a' is perceptible here even through the "contradictions" of the contrasting motif!) However, as a figure in which the primordial theme is re-newed—influenced and heightened, so to speak, by the developmental process—the coda has the same significance as the return of a sonata theme after the development section.[20]

Consequently the likelihood of taking the motif group (bars 2–5) for a theme crystallizes into certainty through the inadequacy of a conflicting interpretation. If this motif group were not "theme," that is, if the first part of the *sostenuto* were likewise preparation for the second theme of the *allegro*, as the second part of the introduction unquestionably is for the main theme, we should have a disposition which corresponds, it is true, to the usual scheme of a sonata movement[21] with an introduction con-

[20] Naturally it can only be a question of a similarity in the cases under comparison. For the primordial theme does not recur in iden-tical form as do the themes in the recapitulation of the sonata move-ment. Neither the harmonic nor the melodic progression of the primordial theme is indicated in the coda. The analogy rests solely on the re-establishment of the original four-bar group. That this analogy is not accidental, but is very important, can be seen from the fact that a correspondence such as that between the first and last entries of motif 'a' also exists between the second (bars 10–11 of the *sostenuto*) and the penultimate (second theme). Attention is more-over called to several "transitional cases" in which themes appear again in the recapitulation in more or less highly changed and very divergent forms; for example, the *largo-allegro* in the first movement of the D minor sonata, Op. 31, No. 2; the main theme of the first movement of the *Eroica*; the beginning of the recapitulation in the first movements of the F minor quartet, Op. 95, and of the A major sonata, Op. 101; and the completely anomalous recapitulation of the *Coriolanus* over-ture, which does not even begin in the main key.

[21] It should be mentioned that Josef Braunstein (5) defines the form of the *Egmont* overture as "a sonata movement without develop-ment section," since he takes the development section for an "epi-logue." "The *Seitensatz* [of the exposition] is followed by the epilogue

taining the thematic material, but one strikingly at variance with the sense of the sonata form. For how could one account for the fact (without the aid of a "poetic idea" at least) that the main theme not only is secondary in importance to the second theme in the preparation, but over

beginning on the first degree of A flat major and containing a melodic motif derived from the main theme, which is then carried on over B flat minor to C minor, in which key the return to the recapitulation begins." Nothing speaks for, and everything against, such a conception. The development section is, of course, unusually short, and up to the C minor section with the entry of the main theme in the bass, it behaves—with its songlike melody and instrumental miniature painting—almost like a lyrical interlude between the highly dramatic exposition and recapitulation, even though the hammered *fortes* of the cadential closes fall between. And this may explain not only Braunstein's erroneous conception of this section, but also how Marx came (22, p. 135) to take it for a "second *Seitensatz*."

Moreover, it is difficult to see just why the quality of a development section should be denied to a section developed by thematic elaboration and lying between an exposition (concluded distinctly enough by an organ point) and an analogous recapitulation. By assuming an epilogue beginning after this organ point, Braunstein is faced with the dilemma of having to allot to the recapitulation a closing group "which from the melodic point of view contains other material than that of the exposition" (p. 150). However, this presumable "epilogue" of the recapitulation is in fact the coda of the whole sonata movement. (If one applies Braunstein's terminology of "coda" to the F major final theme of the overture, then one must differentiate between the "coda of the overture" and the "coda of the F minor movement in sonata-form."

Quite apart from the fact that Braunstein's construction disregards the analogy of exposition and recapitulation, he also ignores at the same time the purport of a closing group, i.e., close of the exposition (or also of the recapitulation where it often widens to the "coda"). From the harmonic point of view, a closing group, as conclusion of the exposition, has to confirm the tonality of the *Seitensatz* but not to modulate, as does the development section, here and everywhere! In the *Egmont* overture, the only part that can be taken for an "epilogue" (if the term is necessary to designate a section such as that on page ooo of this essay) is the appendage to the *Seitensatz*, which brings the exposition and recapitulation to a close on an organ point and is distinguished from the second theme by going back motivically to the *Hauptsatz* (bars 23–24) developed from the eighth-note motif in bars 13–14 and 50 ff of the *allegro*).

and above this is completely eliminated in the coda? And how, on the other hand, could this preferential treatment of the second theme in introduction and coda be reconciled with the fact that the customary tonality equivalence with the main theme is denied it in the recapitulation? By assuming the "primordial theme," on the contrary, we find an individual structure that logically fulfills its own law.

Moreover, the statement of a carrying theme of the sonata form before opening the real sonata exposition is a feature that the *Egmont* overture shares with the two great overtures *Leonore* No. 2 and *Leonore* No. 3, as Braunstein (5) has already emphasized.[22] But the similar form idea serves in both cases as point of departure for quite different structures.

In the *Leonore* overtures the second theme of the *allegro* is identical with the beginning of the Florestan aria quoted in the *adagio*. It is a variant, which as regards its formal construction might be characterized as symphonically instrumental and a proper *allegro* version of an originally vocal *adagio* melody.[23] The second theme of the *Egmont* overture, on the contrary, is not a variant of the theme we hear at the opening of the *sostenuto*, but a new figure developed from the germ motif of the primor-

[22] True, he bases his comparison on an entirely different point of view. "The *Egmont* overture on the one hand and the *Leonore* overtures No. 2 and No. 3 on the other present an interesting analogy in the relationship of the introductory *adagio* to the *allegro* section. In all three overtures, the material of the *adagio* is interwoven with the *allegro* section and made an organic part of it."

[23] A special confirmation of this identity is afforded by a comparison of the versions of the last entry of the theme in *Leonore* No. 2 (*adagio* before the *tempo primo*) and *Leonore* No. 3 (at the conclusion of the recapitulation before the transition to the *presto*), which is also instructive from a historical and a creative-psychological point of view.

dial theme, a product of thematic elaboration, which naturally also undergoes a change in tempo.[24]

The comparison brings out the peculiarity of the form in the *Egmont* overture. The logical development of the primordial theme, as demonstrated above (note 20) represents in its consistency and symmetrical layout a well-ordered and inherently comprehensible structural process, which (beginning outside its ground plan, penetrating it, and extending beyond its recapitulation) overlaps the sonata form as it were, and at the same time rounds it out. The primordial theme is integrated in the sonata texture in the place and the configuration of the second theme; and it completes the sonata structure in the form and function of a coda. The sonata movement, on the other hand, is already interwoven with the opening deployment of the primordial theme through the forerunner of its main theme, and forces this independent structural process to assume a sonatalike continuation as regards order of entry and thematic treatment. Accordingly the form of the F minor movement of the *Egmont* overture seems a synthesis of two structural processes: a typical (sonata) form and one invented *ad hoc*. (The introduction here must be thought of as divided between the two.)

This interpretation, which does not dissect the form into its concrete, co-ordinated parts, but distinguishes interacting "components," also provides an answer to the still pending question as to why the second theme fails to appear in the main key, or its variant in the major mode, in the recapitulation. In the process of the progressive

[24] That the Florestan melody also has to undergo thematic elaboration in the introductions of the two *Leonore* overtures (like the primordial theme in the *sostenuto* of the *Egmont* overture) in no way alters the fundamental difference of the two processes.

development of the primordial theme, culminating in the coda, the second theme forms merely a passing stadium. But since the return to the main key represents a close of the harmonic motion, it would be nonsensical at this point before the thematic development were completed. On the other hand, the sonata form, if we are to think of it only as "component," i.e., without structural independence, needs no tonal rounding off of its own within the form as a whole. And so the final reinstatement of the main key is transferred logically[25] from the recapitulation to the coda, which is not only the end phase of the development of the primordial theme but also the final result of the entire thematic process—the last link in the structural whole.[26]

[25] The fact that the recapitulation begins according to rule in the tonic key and remains in it throughout the entire *Hauptsatz* also has its good reasons; the role of the *Hauptsatz* is finished in the recapitulation. If one recalls the comparison drawn between the coda and the repetition of a theme in the recapitulation (as shown on page 94), one could attribute to each of the two themes a separate exposition and recapitulation and the themes themselves—the effective compass of the one bounded and overlapped by that of the other—become the germinating power of the dramatic structure.

[26] The "open" close on the dominant, which effects a seamless connection with the Victory Symphony, naturally does not destroy the tonal homogeneity of the movement. It occurs in a prolonging cadence of the already established main key and, viewed from the standpoint of harmony, rests solely on the prolongation of one cadence link beyond the limits of the movement. Since the D flat major chord also belongs to the key of F minor as "tonic representative" (VI degree), the modulation in the coda represents, in retrospect, a great F minor cadence. Moreover, the organic connection of the F minor movement does not as yet conclude with the "sword thrust." To this also belongs the rest for the entire orchestra (*Generalpause*), which represents the silence resulting from shock (see also Beethoven's marginal note quoted by Braunstein: "Death could be expressed by a full rest") and the following f of the clarinet and bassoon as expected tonic. At the same time this tonic, in the shape of the mystic woodwind movement that brings the change to the apotheosis, initiates a new F minor cadence, the dominant of which, prolonged by a *fermata*, is

Conversely, since the recapitulation deviates from the main key, the necessity of the succeeding coda is also motivated by the progression of the parts. By bringing the form back to the two indicated components, each one of which represents a logical disposition, we may perhaps have found the independent law, that is, the special structural principle that prompts and premises the individual character of the configuration (*Gestaltung*). At all events it brings out a principle of which the form can be considered the realization.

True, the avoidance of the main key in the *Seitensatz* of the recapitulation can also be explained—independent of the aforesaid viewpoint of a synthetic form—on the score of compositional logic and artistic economy as soon as the Victory Symphony is also taken into consideration as a calculated part of the "whole" in the total plan of the overture. (Since the *Seitensatz* is little suited for a variant in minor mode, only the major variant needs to be considered here.) In the first place, an F major section of the recapitulation, which in a normal harmonic plan should also include the closing group, would have required a correspondingly broader layout of the F minor key necessary for the conclusion of the movement, and perhaps also a broader modulation to the F minor; that is, a very much larger layout for the coda. However, such a disposition (of which the first movement of the C minor symphony furnishes an example) was incompatible with the intention to conclude the overture with the Victory Symphony. Further, the Victory Symphony would have lost the elementary effect of its unexhausted key if the F major

continued through the first eight bars of the Victory Symphony, then to end in F major.

had been anticipated in the F minor movement. But above all, a restlessly shifting modulation curve (from the already attained F major back to F minor and then back again to F major) would have resulted if the recapitulation ended in F major instead of the homogeneous rectilinear harmonic progression F minor–F major (see footnote 26). And finally the idea is not entirely out of the way that the tone colors available in F major would not have been found suitable for the intended color of the *Seitensatz*.[27]

If this would seem to dispose of the theory of the "two components" as a reason for the harmonic progression of the recapitulation, it is by no means untenable. On the contrary, it can only increase our admiration of the systematic unity of the "whole" to find that the character of a part seems determined by the layout of the whole in two ways. Moreover, the theory of the "two components" claims to be merely an hypothesis, an attempt to find a common denominator for the observed structural characteristics. And even if it should sound a trifle far-fetched at first, this is only due to the fact that the question has been approached purely from the angle of form. How obvious it really is will be shown by the following:

For Beethoven the sonata form (with or without introduction, with or without modification) was the

[27] If the evasion of the main key in the *Seitensatz* of the recapitulation proves to be an artistic necessity, this almost automatically answers the additional question why D flat major has become the key of the section. After employing the parallel key for the *Seitensatz* of the exposition, the next related key is that of the VI degree (see footnote 26) which is furthermore related to the key of the *Seitensatz* of the exposition as tonic to dominant. (The customary reference to the relationship of keys a third apart [*Terzverwandschaft*] would be merely a matter of terminology rather than an explanation. For a definition of "tonic relationships," see Klatte (17, p. 278–79).

"given," most manifest one for an overture. In the project of the *Egmont* overture, the dramatic "conflict of two principles"—in the sonata sense—probably coincided from the very beginning with the antithesis Egmont—Alba and the conflict of the two peoples represented by the two figures. In addition to this fundamental movement plan (resulting perhaps from the intention, in advance, of causing a tragic shock by means of an "introduction"), there was also the idea of bringing out clearly the "Alba principle" as cause and motive power of the tragedy and, to this end, of letting the corresponding theme anticipate the sonatalike representation of the conflict. After he had once decided upon an introduction in which not the shadow of an approaching tragic event but the tragic *Agens* should appear directly in the form of a tremendous fully developed theme, the resultant structural problem could have been handled as in the two great *Leonore* overtures. But Beethoven does not repeat himself. He found a new way of incorporating the special form idea in the ordinary movement plan of a sonata with introduction, the aforesaid interweaving of the sonata *allegro* with the development of the theme stated in the *sostenuto*.

At all events, as Lenz felt (21),[28] the *sostenuto* is not related to the *allegro* in the ordinary sense of a preparation for the main "subject." This introduction, which begins with the statement of a theme in order to prepare a

[28] "Not a chorale [in contradiction to Hoffmann's interpretation] and even less an introduction in the narrower sense." And then he continues somewhat abstrusely: "A Cyclopean arched portal, the thematic monogram of the idea differing from the dramatic treatment of the *allegro* as charcoal to brush. The identicalness of the *sostenuto* and *allegro* due to the fundamental motif of these two movements is the *higher* significance derived from Beethoven's thematic style, which in itself is content."

new theme bearing an important relationship to that already introduced (see pp. 88, 90) leads at once in *medias res*. On the other hand, the sonata form with its tonality not yet rounded off up to the entry of the coda, and with a coda that would be hard to motivate without the *sostenuto*, i.e., from the second theme alone (see page 94) is shown to be structurally dependent, as brought out on page 97. Although distinct in tempo, meter, and defined limits, the two sections, each premising and supplementing the other, represent co-ordinated elements of an organically inseparable structural unit.

But in this thematically interwoven unit, which exceeds the limits of form, the *sostenuto* actually fulfills the task of an exposition of the symphonic drama. Here the two carrying themes of the whole are introduced (primordial theme and main theme of the *allegro*), the one complete as "given fact," the other in process of becoming as a procedure induced by the existing "fact," their causal connection being clearly brought out at the same time. And in the direct contraposition of motif and motif the conflict unrolls which in the dramatic instrumental form is carried out *kat'exochen* and in the sonata form of the *allegro* section is stylized in the contrast of the main and second themes.

So this study has revealed two things to us beyond its original aim. First of all, it has answered our question how the amended picture of the thematic relationships agrees with the established interpretation of the poetic content of the overture. It shows in what way and to what extent an unbiased and careful examination of the thematic structure and formal layout of the composition can help us to grasp a "poetic idea" back of the music that is applicable to the content of Goethe's drama. By attacking the question of the "program" from the side of the music rather than from the presupposéd poetic "theme," it arrives, of course, at no new interpretation, but at a sounder, more valid one. With that, the guiding idea comes out very clearly as one that can be defined musically and abstractly at the same time ("conflict of two principles" with tragic cause and issue and the most precise characterization of the opposing forces), while on the other hand certain parts of the music (the development section, for instance) evade a concrete explanation in the programmatic sense, and they also do not require it. For the "theme," which the music undoubtedly borrowed from the poem, seems to have been transformed into a purely musical idea presented and developed in the terms of real, genuine instrumental music. Or, to be more exact, Beethoven, with supreme artistic insight, abstracted from the content of the poem a "poetic idea" that is equivalent to an independent musical idea. There the *Egmont* overture can also be viewed as a work of pure instrumental music.[29]

[29] To terminate the overture with the Victory Symphony seems to the initiated listener so closely associated with the poetic idea, which demands such a conclusion, that the question arises whether the addition of the F major afterpiece to the F minor movement would not also be plausible even without a programme. Riezler (35) raises this question to answer it in the negative. "The triumphant conclusion after the magnificent and genuinely symphonic evolution of the work is called for by the exegencies of the drama, which at this point itself becomes operatic. . . . This is the reason why concert performances of this overture are never quite satisfactory unless they are in celebration of some special occasion and not merely a number in a programme."

The following objections can be raised to this point of view. By complying with the poet's intentions in thus climaxing the overture with a Victory Symphony, Beethoven, in his art, effects something quite different from Goethe in the drama. With the dream apotheosis, which must be considered the real motivation for concluding the tragedy with the Victory Symphony, Goethe breaks through the dra-

This brings us to the second result of this study: a new and conclusive explanation of the form according to purely musical premises. Taking into account the relationship between the thematic evolution given here and the customary form schema, it replaces the picture of an "inconsistent" sonata movement (in which deviations from the norm must be placed to the credit or the debit of the programme) by the perception of a form, legitimate in itself, in which the sonata disposition is arranged in, and sub-

---

matic reality. However, the problematic in this process has nothing to do with the sphere in which the musician works out poetic inspirations. In principle, Beethoven does nothing more than combine a musical composition of tragic content with a musical composition of triumphant character. If we encounter such a change of mood in a purely instrumental work, we are accustomed to look to the music itself for the "idea" back of it without asking for an extramusical motivation. In the *Egmont* overture we might interpret the change to the closing apotheosis in the same way.

One difference at most could be found in the fact that a process such as the contraposition of two symphonic movements takes the form here of a symphonic movement with an "afterpiece." For the Victory Symphony, in its thematic independence and formal separation from the preceding movement, does not have the size of an independent symphonic movement. It has the distinct character of closing music to accompany the fall of the curtain when the play is over.

Now Beethoven himself furnishes us with an example of pure instrumental music that is very similar to the above: the finale of the string quartet, Op. 95, which dates from the same period. But it is more important to glance at the motivation provided by the overture itself (that is, the manner of introducing the Victory Symphony) than to cite analogous cases. For this we must take into consideration— apart from the tonal or harmonic preparation, which has already been touched on above—not alone the eight mystic woodwind bars at the close of the *allegro*, which really bring about the change and which, parallel with the dramatic action, might be interpreted as the intervention of transcendent powers, but we must furthermore compare the opening of the *allegro con brio* in the overture with the beginning of the closing music to the drama and it will be understood why Beethoven replaced in the overture the two-bar *fortissimo* passage which opens No. 9 of the incidental music, with those eight exciting organ point bars which, in quickened pace, lead from the *pianissimo* to the *fortissimo* of the victory fanfares!

ordinated to, a specially contrived and logical plan. And if an interpretation of the form, which seeks to prove the "structural principle" behind it, still remains merely an interpretation in spite of all efforts to arrive at a convincing underlying principle, it will at least serve as an auxiliary construction in bringing out clearly the homogeneity and logic of the form (*Gestaltung*), and, by so doing, deepen the understanding of the wonderful organism of the work.

CHAPTER VIII

Pseudo and Riddle Canons by Beethoven

An examination of the canons and essays at new solutions

I : THE PSEUDO CANONS

Anyone desiring to acquaint himself more fully with Beethoven's creative work in the field of the canon will be confronted first of all by the difficulty of finding a complete collection of them. Breitkopf and Härtel's Collected Edition of Beethoven's works contains, as we know, only twenty-three canons, eighteen in the main section (really seventeen since No. 3 represents two settings of the same text) and five in the Supplement. Works of this category that have been newly found or which turned up again after this monumental work was published are scattered about in collections of correspondence, in biographies, special publications, etc., while a few recently discovered manuscripts are still unpublished.

A large amount of material is contained and discussed in Thayer's Biography (40), but Frimmel's *Beethoven*

* I am indebted to the Bärenreiter Verlag, Kassel and Basel for permission to reprint this essay from *Musikforschung*, No. ¾, 1950.

Handbuch (7) was the first to present a complete survey, which in the following decade was supplemented by the section "Canons, Musical Jokes, Souvenirs" in Willy Hess's monograph "What Works of Beethoven are missing in the Collected Edition?" (10)

If we set out to explore the field under this guidance, we arrive at the following facts:

1. A number of the works in question appear in different versions, which sometimes contain very manifest errors that cannot be excused on the score of illegibility.

2. Nearly all solutions of the riddle canons need to be rechecked. In three cases, solutions still seem to be wanting altogether.

3. Certain pieces listed as "canons" cannot be identified as such, or lead one to suspect that there is an error.

4. These doubtful cases—which in part have been questioned in Beethoven literature—along with a few other discrepancies between the lists of Frimmel and Hess will explain the surprising and—from the viewpoint of artistic-practical interest—regrettable fact that the number of actually existing canons—in contradistinction to mere sketches, fragments, or pieces either presumably in canon form or so designated in Beethoven literature, has not yet been definitely established.

In the following essay I shall try to examine this material, limiting my investigation to the real vocal canons, i.e., those based on a text. To this end the doubtful pieces must be verified. Questions regarding the notation and manner of execution of a number of the real canons will then be discussed, the riddle canons (those of the Collected Edition and the supplementary ones) being treated as a special group.

Beethoven Studies

1. Examination

According to Frimmel "there are far more than forty known Beethoven canons."[1] That the word "known" should be taken here in a very broad sense is shown by a list of forty-seven canons "compiled according to the text and mostly according to the music." For our inventory we must first of all exclude four on this list (if research does not bring new information to light).

1. The canon *Ein anders ists das erste Jahr* exists in Beethoven's handwriting, but according to Nottebohm,[2] Beethoven merely copied it but did not compose it.

2. A canon *Hier ist das Werk, schafft mir das Geld,* communicated by Karl Holz. Both Frimmel and Hess question its genuineness.

3. A canon *Wie Silber die Rede . . .* which we know only from a passage in the diary of Fanny Giannatasio del Rio (20, 16). Since Frimmel refers to this piece as "written for del Rio" and Hess has taken the title over in his index of the canons, sight unseen so to speak, it is advisable to examine the source. The note reads: "He [Beethoven] once wrote out a little canon for us, only in pencil, on the text: *Wie Silber die Reden doch zu rechter Zeit schweigen ist lauteres Gold* (Speech is silver, but silence at the right moment is pure gold). Now the expressions "he wrote out for us" and especially "only in pencil" are by no means the same thing as "he wrote for us," as Frimmel interprets it. And when one reads the quoted text in

---

[1] Bekker also gives the figure as "not less than approximately 40." Later Schünemann puts the number as "over forty, in fact."

[2] *Zwei Skizzenbücher von Beethoven aus den Jahren 1801–1802.*

its entirety, it will be found that as far as sense is concerned, the beginning of the canon agrees with the Herder text of the well-known riddle canon *Das Schweigen* (No. 5 in the Collected Edition) while the text of the close is identical. Fanny del Rio therefore probably had this in mind and only quoted the text inexactly from memory. Naturally Beethoven could also have composed a variant on the text he had already used once before. But there is no basis for such an assumption. On the contrary, if he really wrote this composition especially for the del Rio family, then Frau Pessial (del Rio's granddaughter) would surely have mentioned it to Thayer in connection with the two pieces written for them. See (40, IV, App. II). The annotation "probably identical with the canon *Das Schweigen*" should therefore be added to the title *Wie Silber die Rede*.

Three further titles are lacking in the alphabetical list of first lines that Frimmel appends to his detailed Index. Besides a canon without text (for de Boer), which does not belong in this section, two pieces are missing, strange to say: one that is not a canon and one that does not appear to be one. The musical joke *Erster aller Tobiasse* contained in a letter to Haslinger has been listed erroneously in Thayer's index (No. 177, Supplement, p. 194) as a four-part canon with reference to the manuscript in St. Petersburg. Frimmel then took it over from here in his index. As the graph of the three-part piece in Thayer's biography shows (Vol. v, p. 393) it is not a canon, although evolved perhaps from the idea for a canon. Hess also does not list it as a canon but as a "fragment." And the piece, *Glaube und Hoffe*, listed among the "Five Canons" in the Supplement to the Collected Edition is also not a canon in the four-part form in which it appears there—and in Beethoven's manuscript! Why it nevertheless belongs with the canons will be brought out later.

Of the forty-one titles to which we have now reduced Frimmel's list, twenty-three have already appeared in the Collected Edition. Of the remaining eighteen, the following four are to be verified:

1. *Ich küsse Sie*
2. *Bernardus*
3. *Sanct Petrus*
4. *Wir irren allesamt*

In addition to these "dubious" ones from Frimmel's index, there are the following titles listed by Hess and expressly designated as canons. Of these the first two are mentioned by Frimmel, though they are not listed in his index:

5. Canon on a garbled verse from Faust
6. *Fettlümmerl* ...
7. Canon on Germany's revolt
8. Canon on the text *Te solo adoro*
9.   "   "

Ich kuesse Sie

Ich küs-se sie drük-ke sie an mein Herz

Ich der Haupt - mann der Haupt-mann

EXAMPLE 47

The two lines of melody given in Beethoven's letter of January 6, 1816, to Anna Milder-Hauptmann are listed as a canon by both Frimmel and Hess. The latter's more precise indication "a-3" is presumably based on Riemann's interpretation (40, III, p. 537).

We must next mention that the notation, even after the discovery of the manuscript, which led to the correction of the previously printed versions, was published in two different versions.[3] For while Kalischer (13, III, No. 503), who discovered the manuscript, reported that the second line "was written in a hastily sketched F clef (bass), Riemann goes on to say that "the second line surely ought to be also in the tenor clef as counterpoint of the first; perhaps canonic imitation of the first part was intended, the whole therefore being one of the Master's many little canons written in albums or in letters."

EXAMPLE 48

(In the second bar of the bass, the quarter note of the original version has been changed to a half note). It is difficult to understand how the great theorist could have been led into this three-part monstrosity and claim that Beethoven really intended this impossible *Satz*. That the

[3] Apart from the fact that in many of the later reprints the repeat mark, which the earlier editions gave at the end of the second staff, has been retained. The ♯ before the second line in the corrected version given in Prelinger's edition of Beethoven's correspondence (31, Supplement) can only be a typographical error.

second line of the musical passage in the letter (no matter in what version) is not a counterpoint to the first[4] is just as clear as the harmonic absurdity of the canonic imitation of the first line (dominant of G with tonic C as close or repetition).

If one is absolutely determined to experiment with this musical passage in the letter, more useful results can be obtained by taking each line by itself. The first line can be imitated in contrary motion in reasonable harmony. There is only the harshness of the anticipation at the repetition of the first voice, which cannot be helped.

Ich küs-se sie   drük-ke sie an mein Herz   Ich küs-se sie

EXAMPLE 49

The second line could be imitated canonically at the third below (or the sixth above). The $\sharp$ in parentheses produces Kalischer's version transposed to the same key.

EXAMPLE 50

But it is unlikely that Beethoven intended this little pleasantry. There is no need to imagine some secret behind a

---

[4] Because only very slight changes were necessary in order to bring the parts into contrapuntal relationship!

conceit of a playful moment, such as this—and all the less so since the repeat signs in the second staff, which appeared in the early editions, seem to be missing in the manuscript.[5] So one can delete this from the list of canons without losing any of Beethoven's genius.

Sanct Petrus . . . Bernardus

In a letter to Privy Councillor Peters (40, IV, p. 189), Beethoven wrote: "What are you doing? Are you well or ill? How's your wife? Allow me to sing you something."

EXAMPLE 51

That these two staves are not canons is apparent on the face of it.[6] Very probably they are quotations from two canons which were known to the recipient of the letter. In the Conversation-book of January, 1820 (27, p. 258, 315), Peters wrote: "Too bad about your canon, it is perhaps already faded out. It would have immortalized me." And a later entry reads in a similar vein: "The two lovely canons are surely faded out by now. St. Peter is a rock. One must build on this!"

In Thayer's biography (40, IV, p. 191) the explanation

[5] In fact, Kalischer recommended a facsimile copy.

[6] They can naturally be worked out as canons as a joke—the first at the third below after two quarter notes, the second at a third above after four half notes.

of the letter referred to in the Conversation-book is followed by a sketch of a three-part composition on the words: *"Sanct Petrus ist der Fels, auf diesen kann man bauen. . . ."* This "little piece, the notes of which are difficult to interpret but which is not worked out as a canon" employs the above motif with the lower voice in imitation. It was thus a preliminary step or parergon of the canons mentioned in the Conversation-book to which the letter ostensibly referred. Since these compositions, which were missing at that time, have not been found in the meantime, the titles *Sanct Petrus* and *Bernardus* are only of biographical interest.

Wir irren allesamt . . .

The little piece *Wir irren allesamt, nur jeder irret anders* has come down to us in two different renderings, one of which (in the violin clef) is not in Beethoven's hand. The other, which was added to a dictated letter of Beethoven's, is quoted by Deiters (40, v, p. 418), after a

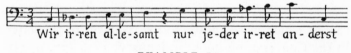

Wir ir-ren al-le-samt   nur je-der ir-ret an-derst

EXAMPLE 52

copy by Otto Jahn.[7] "Nohl is right in seeing that the present is not a canon," said Deiters with reference to Nohl's title *Reconciliation Canon*. He then goes on: "If the above reading is correct, then with entry one bar later it can perhaps pass as a two-in-one canon at the

[7] There are two printed versions of each. For one see Thayer's index and Kalischer (13, v, No. 1180); for the other, Kalischer (13, v, No. 1196), who follows Nohl by making the third quarter note of the second bar an *f* instead of a *g*.

unison." Riemann's joy in discovery has led him astray in this instance.[8] Neither does his suggestion produce a serviceable canon nor could Beethoven be said to have written a barely "passable canon," if writing a canon had been his intention. Thus insofar as all notations known up to now are concerned, *Wir irren allesamt* is not a canon.

Canon on a garbled verse from Faust

In Hess's index we find under No. 22: "Canon on a garbled verse from Faust. Unpublished. Mentioned in Frimmel's *Neue Beethoveniana*." In his *Handbuch*, Frimmel himself referred to such a canon in the *Neue Beethoveniana*, but, as already mentioned, he did not include the title in his index. The *Neue Beethoveniana* (new edition 1890, p. 341) mentions it only briefly in the following footnote:

About 1825 Beethoven drafted a canon on the garbled verse from Faust: *Uns geht es cannibalisch wohl, wie fünfhundert Säuen. Nohl* III, p. 645.

The data in Nohl's biography, however, is limited to the statement that "further volumes of a previously mentioned sketchbook (of 1825) contained sketches of canons, one on the childlike verse *Freu dich des Lebens*, and another on the garbled verse from Faust: *"Uns geht es cannibalisch wohl, wie fünfhundert Säuen!"* That is all that the quoted sources have to say on the subject.

One gets exact—and divergent—information from an unquoted authority. In Nottebohm's article, "Six Sketch-

---

[8] It was really Riemann who first discovered the canon *Es muss sein*, or rediscovered it (in vindication of tradition) by identifying it as a canon, contrary to Deiters (40, v, 302). The canon is now generally known in Riemann's notation.

books from the years 1825 and 1826," in the *Zweite Bee-thoveniana* (p. 11), we find: "Among the sketches for the fugue, Op. 130, there is the following passage:

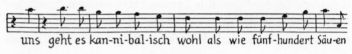

uns geht es kan-ni-bal-isch wohl als wie fünf-hundert Säu-en

EXAMPLE 53

Nottebohm adds : "If we do not take all these notes exactly as they are written and venture to make a slight change, we obtain a two-in-one canon at the unison. Perhaps that was also the intention."

Here a distinction is made with scientific exactness between an objective fact (the sketch as it stands) and an assumption regarding it. And more than the assumption that "perhaps a canon was the intention" cannot be deduced from it. To simply index it as a "sketch for a canon" is going a step too far.

Fettlümmerl . . .

Frimmel also omitted this 'unpublished canon' in his index, although he cited it as "mentioned, without notes, in Kalischer's edition of the correspondence."[9] Quoting the same source, Hess lists it as an unpublished canon under No. 23, and in the appendix refers to the published sketches which appeared in the meantime. These were the entries in the *Beethoven Haus-und Jahreskalendar* of 1823, which Schünemann examined and published. According to the latter, the "already badly faded notation"

9 Kalischer (13, IV, p. 324) makes only the following comment on it (in connection with a letter from Beethoven to his brother Johann): "In these scandalous times Beethoven seems to have taken his musical revenge through the canon *Fettlümmerl Bankert haben triumphiert.*"

of the intended three-part canon which "is already barely decipherable" is only a fragment (six bars as compared with a rhythmical sketch of ten bars with accompanying text) and naturally cannot be solved canonically.

If Schünemann also reckoned on the possible discovery of other sketches, we can only state for the time being that the canon, which perhaps was never entirely written out, does not exist.

Canon on Germany's Revolt

Among the still unpublished canons mentioned by Hess as having been discovered by Unger in a private Swiss Beethoven collection (Bodmer Collection, Zürich) is one called *Canon on Germany's Revolt* (No. 39 in the index). The source quoted is Unger's article, "Beethoven's Unpublished Music," in the *Zeitschrift für Musik*, November, 1935 (45).

Unger does not mention such a title in his article. Hess seems to have chosen it according to his own interpretation for a "fresh little piece of unaccompanied vocal music on the text *Geschlagen ist der Feind*, which Unger found among the 1814 sketches." That the interpretation is wrong can be seen from Unger's catalogue of the aforesaid collection (1939). There under Mh. 87 we find: "Two sheets of sketches for the Battle of Victoria (Part II) and an unknown canon on the words *Geschlagen ist der Feind*."

Te solo adoro . . .

As Unger states in his article, he "deciphered a number of lines written very indistinctly in lead pencil, as two canons on the text *Te solo adoro,* none of which coincide with the canon on the same text published in the Collected Edition. One learns from the catalogue of the Bodmer Collection (44) that it is a question of "approximately finished sketches." Therefore these can be accepted only with reservations for our "stocktaking" and must therefore be put aside for the moment.

Other canonic sketches and a questionable notation
The following indications will indemnify the canon votary for the loss of so many presumable canons.

The beginning of a letter to Haslinger from 1826 (?) (46, No. 99) can be imitated at the unison at the distance of one bar.

EXAMPLE 54

The motifs given in a letter to Hauschka in 1818 (40, IV, p. 99) also permit canonic imitation, the one (which Beethoven follows immediately with the comes and to which

EXAMPLE 55

he later adds a counterpoint) at the unison at the distance

EXAMPLE 56

of one bar; the other at the fifth below at the distance of one bar, possibly also on the fourth above at the distance of half a bar. But naturally these are not really fragments of canons but conceits evolved from Beethoven's contrapuntal thinking. A little one-part composition, which Nohl (*Neue Briefe Beethovens*, p. 83–84) quotes from a sketchbook (to the *Glorreichen Augenblick*) as presumable illustration to a letter to Archduke Rudolf will possibly turn up as a canon some day. In Nohl's version it does not admit of solution as a canon. But it may not be correct.

THE STOCK

After eliminating the pseudo canons or compositions existing only in the sketch stadium, we come down to the following real and finished canons by Beethoven, in addition to those listed in the Collected Edition:

Printed (r=*Riddle Canons*)

1. *Ars longa, vita brevis* (for Hummel)   R
2. *Ars longa, vita brevis* (for Sir George Smart)   R
3. *Glück fehl' dir vor allem* . . .
4. *Brauchle-Linke*
5. *Das Schöne zu dem Guten* (for Rellstab)   R
6. *Bester Herr Graf, Sie sind ein Schaf!*
7. *Gott ist eine feste Burg*   R
8. *Es muss sein* . . .
9. *Gehabt euch wohl*
10. *Tugend ist kein leerer Name*
11. *Falstaff, Falstaff, lass dich sehen*
12. *Doktor sperrt das Thor dem Tod* . . .
13. *Ich war hier*
14. *Hol euch der Teufel! B'hüt euch Gott!*   R

Unprinted

15. *Bester Magistrat ihr friert* (facsimile published)
16. *Geschlagen ist der Feind*
17. *Herr Graf, ich komme Sie zu fragen*

Therefore the number of existing canons, including the twenty-three given in the Collected Edition, is exactly forty. Of these, the following are printed in open score (in *partitura*):

> *Falstafferl*, five part, published by Kalischer in *Die Musik*, Vol. II, No. 3, and in (13, IV, No. 905)
>
> *Es muss sein*, four part, given in Thayer (40, V, p. 302) in Riemann's version.
>
> *Gehabt euch wohl* and *Tugend ist kein leerer Name*, both three part, published by Schünemann.

The following are in close score, but ready for use:

> *Glück fehl' dir vor allem* (40, IV, p. 521) four part canon at the unison, each part entering at the distance of one bar.
>
> *Brauchle-Linke* (Thayer Index, App. No. 263) also four part canon at the unison, each entry indicated at a distance of two bars.
>
> *Ich war hier*, apart from facsimile reproductions printed in (15, No. 1304) and in open score in (42), two part canon at the fifth below, entry at the distance of one bar.

The texts of two canons require critical examination: Kalischer published *Bester Herr Graf* (13, IV, No. 874) in an incorrect version, which was taken over verbatim by Prelinger (V, No. 1280) and Thayer (40, IV, p. 389). In Kalischer the alto clef is obviously wrong. Deiters, who reproduces the composition in Thayer (40) based on a copy of the autograph which he made himself, gives the tenor clef as it should be and the key signature B flat, which is wanting in Kalischer. But despite this the canon does not admit of solution in this reading. If one consults the facsimile of the manuscript that was written with pencil in a café (in Hirschbach's *Repertorium*, p. 468) and published by Schindler, it will be found that Kalischer read two notes wrong and Deiters three.

The first note in bar 6 (given correctly by Kalischer) is distinctly a *g*, not an *f*, as Deiters read it. One can see the reason for the other errors. The fourth note of bar 7 is undoubtedly a *c*, not an *e*, as with Deiters (or a *g*, as with Kalischer), but there is a note-shaped spot just above the *c* on the *e* line of the staff that could also be taken for a note (correction?) although the dot appertaining to it is missing. That the correct note is *c* and not *e* is shown by the fact that from an *e* to the *d* of the following bar, we should have parallel octaves or unisons with bars 1 and 2. Deiters reads the fourth note of bar 5 as *g* (Kalischer also) because a ledger line seems to pass through the note and there is only the suggestion of a ledger line visible underneath it. But it cannot be a *g* since it is much higher than the three previous *a*'s written in a line. Besides, a *g* would no more agree with the harmony than a *b♭*, for which the note might be taken. Thus a *c* is evidently meant, the upper ledger line (which should be underneath the note) being a little out of position. In addition, the letter *c* has been written underneath the note in a strange hand (Schindler?) in order to identify it.[10]

After the notation has been clarified, the little piece is easily solved as a four part canon at the unison. The entries of the parts (after every two bars) are shown in the facsimile.

Bes-ter Herr Graf Sie sind ein Schaf

EXAMPLE 57

The parts are so written that when read one after the other they give the theme of the canon.[11]

Doktor sperrt das Thor dem Tod . . .

In the version of this canon in Thayer (40, v, p. 196) and Kalischer (No. 1069)[12] (according to Nottebohm's text published in the Leipzig *Allgemeine Musilkalische Zeitung* of March 2, 1870), bar 12 has the note *a*. That

[10] In bar 3, a note has also been identified in the same way.

[11] Max Unger called my attention to his *Neue Beethoven Studien* (42) after the above article was written. In this is found the canon *Bester Herr Graf*, written in open score, in a revised reading, in which two wrong notes of earlier editions (in bars 6 and 7) have been corrected. The third error (bar 5) escaped Unger's notice, and the harmonic discrepancy resulting therefrom may be the real reason for his assumption that the accidental, which is written very distinctly in bar 4, is presumably a typographical error which should be replaced by a natural. After correcting the note in question in bar 5, this no longer holds good.

[12] Nottebohm's rendering agrees with that of Kalischer and Kastner-Kapp (No. 1288). Strange to say, however, they refer to Nohl's first edition, not to Nottebohm.

must be a mistake since the note *a* changes the sound of the tonic (at which the other sections of the melody aim) into the six-four chord of the parallel tonic. Even if we hear it more "horizontally" than "vertically" and find the note *a* charming in being melodically logical and a deviation into the parallel (so long as the canon does not come to a close), it is still difficult to believe that Beethoven would have written the passage in this way. The note *a*, which seems to be the correct one here, is found in the version given by Kalischer in his *Neue Beethovenbriefe* (p. 188) along with another variant in the penultimate bar—but he dropped it again in the Collected Edition of the letters. Strange to say, in both cases he refers to the same authority: Nottebohm's publication of the letter in which the canon appears (to Dr. Braunhofer, dated May 13, 1825).

Moreover there are still two more printed variants of the canon, one by Nohl (No. 335) and the other by Prelinger (III, No. 875)—both apparently incorrect. Since the manuscript, according to Frimmel, is owned by the Gesellschaft der Musikfreunde in Vienna and Hess states that a facsimile appeared in the supplement of the *Wiener Telegraph*, No. 2, 1838,[13] a critical revision of the text should be possible. Apart from establishing the correct or most convincing reading, the canon presents no problem. The entries of the four voices (perhaps meant to be at the unison but naturally also possible with imitation at the octave below) are indicated.

As regards the unpublished pieces, Unger, under the

---

[13] Kastner is the only one who makes reference to this facsimile, although he does not mention the date. Perhaps Nohl, with his indefinite comment on the letter ("moreover already printed") had the facsimile in mind.

index number Mh-38 of the aforementioned catalogue, has the following to say with regard to No. 15 on our list: "It is a canon at the unison for four bass voices with accompaniment of string basses, E major." We have already spoken of No. 16. Hess has the following to say with regard to No. 17: "Unger has brought to light another unknown canon (C major, 4/4 time, three part); it seems to have reference to Smeskall and begins with the words *Herr Graf, ich komme Sie zu fragen, wie Sie sich befinden,* etc. The piece is fully worked out." (According to the preface, he evidently refers to a personal communication from Unger.)

II : THE RIDDLE CANONS

Lerne schweigen . . .

This riddle canon, which (without solution) is given in the Collected Edition, was solved soon after its first publication. But to prevent this solution—which Beethoven certainly saw and apparently accepted—from being supplanted by a new and incorrect one, we must call attention to a strange oversight on the part of Beethoven research. In the section, "Compositions of the year 1815," in Vol. iii of the German edition of Thayer, there is a solution introduced by the following sentence: "The solution of the canon *Lerne schweigen* is found in a sketch (28, ii, p. 330) with entry of the second part after one bar at the fifth below, and the third part after three bars at the octave below." The reference to the "key" in the form of a Beethoven sketch would lead the reader to suppose that this was the first, newly found solution. But this solution does not sound satisfactory. We must disagree with one point while two others are questionable.

1. The signature of F major—without transposition of the melody—is replaced by that of B flat major, because a precise imitation at the fifth below would require the note e^b. In point of fact, Beethoven's sketch has an e^b in bar 2 of the inner voice. But here one naturally cannot simply transfer this signature to the *proposta* notated in F major.

2. The rendering of the melody in bar 3 differs from that of the Collected Edition, without the source of the new version being given.

3. It seems doubtful whether a correct solution would permit imitations at irregular entry periods.

Since the canon (according to Nottebohm's Thematic Index) was composed at the end of 1815, written in C. Neafe's album on January 24, 1816, and published on March 6, 1817, in the supplement of the Vienna *Allgemeine Musikalische Zeitung*, Thayer (40, IV, p. 77) therefore includes it in the list of the 1817 compositions with the accompanying comment: "In the supplement of Kanne's *Allgemeine Musikalische Zeitung* of March 6, 1817 (with Payer's solution)." But Thayer's index (No. 202) and Nohl (*Neue Briefe Beethovens*, p. 104, note to No. 130) already referred to Payer's solution!

The first edition of the riddle canon in the aforementioned magazine brings out the surprising fact that the entry signs are indicated, which Beethoven apparently considered necessary, since the imitations should really occur at irregular periods (as in the aforesaid solution); and that there is a b^b with a natural alongside it above the melodic note b^b in bar 2 (which in the inner voice, in bar 2, should be an e^b, according to the sketch). Both indications are omitted in the text of the Collected Edition, which, so far as the notes go, agrees with the first edition, but differs from it in the tempo indication and in the absence of expression marks.[14]

The solution published in the issue of June 5 bears the following proud title: "Solution of the riddle canon of Herr L. van Beethoven/See No. 10 of this Supplement No. 3/and an absolutely correct one by Herr Hyronimus Payer." It is naturally in F major, only it has the note e^b in the inner voice in the aforementioned bar and sounds perfectly natural and spontaneous. There is also no record that Beethoven ever objected to it. It is amusing to read underneath Payer's composition: "Herr Payer clothes the textual solution of the same in the following interesting composition [here follows a four-part riddle canon with four solutions to the text]: Herr van Beethoven's canon is at the fifth below and at the octave." Signed: Hyronimus Payer. Payer's canon is moreover printed in Thayer's index.

Si non per portas . . .

There are three published versions of this riddle canon. According to Riemann (40, v, p. 249) the version of the Collected Edition

Si non per Por-tas per mu-ros per mu-ros per mu-ros

EXAMPLE 58

which is probably the only correct one, permits two satisfactory solutions of the canon: one at the second above in contrary motion

---

[14] The first edition has *poco sostenuto* instead of the *assai sostenuto* of the Collected Edition, and in the penultimate bar a *pp* leading gradually to the *forte* in the last bar.

EXAMPLE 59

and one at the third above in similar motion, the entry sign also taking in the rest.

EXAMPLE 60

As the graphs show, there is an error in the explanation. The canon at the second above is in similar motion, that on the third above in contrary motion. (Moreover, the original notation in Thayer is incorrect since the signature is lacking.) Riemann's solutions might pass as unobjectionable in the technical sense, but they are unsatisfactory from the musical point of view. It is hard to believe that Beethoven intended the canon in this way.

It is rewarding to try to find a new solution (first for the rendering given in the Collected Edition). The entry of the imitative voice at the fourth above results in a harmonically logical progression, but in bar 3 postulates a movement out of the octave to the unison that represents an uncanonic pseudo unison, which would be objectionable from an artistic, compositional viewpoint. To remedy this, instead of imitation at the fourth, imagine a fugal "tonal" answer, which at the beginning lets the V degree correspond with the I, in bar 3 passes over to a real transposition to the fifth, and towards the end (on the Bach model—see *Wohltemperiertes Klavier*, I, fugues in E flat major and B minor) effects the return modulation. Moreover the prolongation of the dominant, which is achieved by this change in the third bar, obviates the danger of a false relation in the following bar.

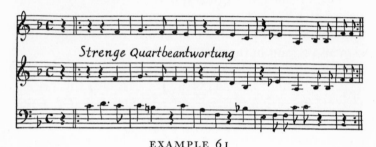

EXAMPLE 61

Fugue-like "tonal" answer with return modulation

Of the other two versions, that of Nohl (also taken over by Kastner)[15] is doubtful and can therefore be disregarded. Unger's, on the other hand (46, No. 119), ranks with that of the Collected Edition since, like Nohl (see footnote 15) he interprets the second quarter note of bar 3 as *g*. According to the facsimile, the note—which is not written exactly on the line—can just as well be taken for a *g* as for an *f*. But when in doubt we must take the most probable ,which is Unger's setting. It permits the simplest and most flowing solution of the canon, which reads as follows in strict imitation at the fourth:

EXAMPLE 62

[15] Nohl takes the first quarter note of bar 3 for '*bb*.' Apart from

Glaube und hoffe

The version of this composition written on a commemorative leaf for the younger Schlesinger (22) and included among the canons of the Collected Edition[16] is not a canon but a composition in free imitative style in which none of the three upper voices are precise canonic imitations of the motif introduced by the bass. For this reason Thayer (40, IV, p. 176) takes care to call it only a "canonlike composition." But in his letter to Beethoven of July 3, 1822, Maurice Schlesinger wrote: "I honour as a sacred relic the beginning of a canon that was given me at that time." The bass furnishes the solution of this riddle.

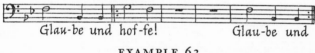

EXAMPLE 63

That is really the "beginning of a canon," although Beethoven concealed this meaning by adding a freer texture. The following four graphs will serve to illustrate this:

the fact that the facsimile of the manuscript (in Marx) shows *a* fairly distinctly, the following *f♭*, as fourth quarter note, is written higher up and the flat, which expressly cancels the natural in the previous bar, argues against the first quarter note being a *b♭*. With regard to the second quarter note, which Nohl reads as *g*, see above.

[16] The version of Kalischer (13, IV, No. 775) and Prelinger (31, II, No. 618) deviates from that of the Collected Edition in the soprano of the penultimate bar. The version in the Collected Edition was based on a copy by Nottebohm. In the facsimile the passage is ambiguous. The question, however, does not interest us here.

EXAMPLE 64

Das Schöne zu dem Guten

The canon written as a souvenior for Rellstab (not to be confused with that on the same text written on a commemorative sheet for Maria Pachler-Koschak[17] has appeared in print at various times (40, v, p. 209), but a solution never seems to have been published; at least one seeks it in vain in the better-known works. At the first glance

[17] Thomas San Galli (36, p. 448, 372) also confused them.

an imitation at the unison beginning on the fourth quarter note of bar 1 seems possible. But Beethoven could not have intended such a simple canon, and he cannot have wished to make things so easy for the recipient. Perhaps the following is a reasonable solution: besides the imitation at the unison, two others at the second above on the second quarter note of each bar, seems possible.

EXAMPLE 65

Harmonically still more plausible perhaps (on account of the stronger tonic), but somewhat more daring (because of hidden parallel fifths), is a version in which imitation at the second is replaced by imitation at the fourth above. At all events it can be offered for discussion. One can naturally imagine both solutions for mixed voices.

EXAMPLE 66

Ars long, vita brevis

For the shorter of Beethoven's two canons on this text (for Sir George Smart) we will scarcely find a better solution than the simple four-in-one imitation at the unison given by Riemann (40, v, p. 248) or the second that he offers as an alternative (according to a hint from Holz). On the other hand, the older canon on the same text, dedicated to Hummel, seems to represent a temporarily nebulous problem. True, it permits an imitation at the fifth above (at the given entry sign), but we gain little by this. The two-in-one composition from the middle on sounds harmonically unconvincing and, at the end, paltry. And the length and contrasting layout of the theme leads one to assume that it was designed for more than two parts. The futile effort to find a solution makes one suspect that the text, as given in the printed editions, must be incorrect. If Nohl, who published the first edition (*Neue Beethovenbriefe*, No. 133), mentions the owner's name (Hummel's widow), this still does not make it certain that his source was the manuscript itself or a copy of it. And in Thayer's graph (iii, p. 550) reference is made to Nohl's first edition, but the version deviates somewhat from that of the first edition[18] without any source being given for the altered version. So a text revision of this canon is the principal requirement.

Gott is eine feste Burg

Frimmel's comment on this canon is: "considered unsolvable." Hess calls it a three-in-one canon, probably on the basis of the following solution by Riemann (40, v, p. 170, footnote 3): "However, besides the entry indicated by*—at the fourth above—an earlier one at the distance of half a bar (also at the fourth above) is possible so that the composition will be in three parts." Leaving aside the question of the three parts for the moment, among the two-in-one possibilities the imitation at the fourth above,

[18] A whole bar rest is lacking after the first *Ars longa* and the entry sign. The last eighth note in bar 8 is *a*, not *g* as with Nohl.

beginning with the third bar, seems the most obvious.
For first of all, it is in the ear from the beginning of the
Credo of the *Missa Solemnis* (bars 5–8 and the parallel
passage, bars 37–40); secondly, it enters at the given entry
sign; and thirdly, the notation of the theme in the bass
clef seems to reckon with an imitation at a higher pitch.

In addition, the solution is also contained in a Conversation-book of 1825 (the year the canon was written),
as stated by Thayer (40, IV, 343).[19] At all events one can-

Gott ist ei-ne fe-ste Burg   Gott ist

EXAMPLE 67

(Bass clef and signature B flat major are to be
be added. The quarter note in bar 5 is apparently an incorrect reading or a typographical
error.)

not deduce more from this notation than the probability
that Beethoven intended the canon to be carried out in
this way. What speaks against this solution is its harmonic
progression, which robs the transposed theme in the
prominent upper voice of the tonic close of the *proposta*.
For this reason the imitation at the fifth below (in spite of
the tonic entering in bar 4 as fourth) would be preferable.
True, Riemann's second suggestion of having an imitation at the fourth above begin at the second half of the
first bar disregards Beethoven's entry sign, but it is musi-

[19] Strange to say, reference to this passage is lacking in the discussion of the canon in Thayer (40, IV) and vice versa. The notation
from the Conversation-book is mentioned only to characterize the
Credo theme of the *Missa Solemnis,* without further details.

cally plausible. Here the interchange of parts (fifth below for fourth above) might be even more convincing.

The three-in-one version produced by combining both imitations sounds, on the contrary (in any position of the voices), still too unwieldly and far-fetched to be the correct solution,[20] apart from the fact that Beethoven would have indicated the entry of the voices at irregular periods if that had been his intention. If one experiments further with this riddle canon, it will be found that with the given entry sign, a diminution at the octave is possible but can scarcely have been meant as solution. On the other hand, a serviceable solution at the fifth must ignore the entry sign.

Gott ist ei - ne fe-ste Burg Gott ist ei - ne fe-ste

EXAMPLE 68

It seems therefore, that Frimmel's "considered unsolvable" is irrefutable if it is a matter of offering a thoroughly satisfactory solution.

Hol euch der Teufel! B'hüt euch Gott

Hess presents this little piece (in agreement with Thayer's index, No. 220) as "Canon a-2." In any case he bases this on an entry in a Conversation-book of March, 1820, through which the canon has come down to us. There we find written in an unknown hand:[21] "Last sum-

[20] At all events it is best in the following setting: theme upper voice, imitation after a half bar in the inner voice, imitation in the lower voice after two bars.

mer you sent Steiner from Moedling a Canon *infinitus a due*

EXAMPLE 69

No one solved it; I solved it, for it enters at the second

EXAMPLE 70

Hol euch der Teufel! B'hüt euch Gott! was the text. *Es geht in infinitum.*" We do not know Beethoven's reply to the writer of these lines or whether he perhaps completed verbally the solution presented to him. Be that as it may, we can assert that the canon can be carried out in two ways as a four-in-one:

1. After every two bars the third and fourth voices take over the theme in contrary motion, the third entering at the third above (tenth) to the first; the fourth at the octave to the second:

EXAMPLE 71

2. In similar motion, so that the third voice at a third above runs parallel with the first, the fourth at the sixth above, with the second:

[21] Quoted from Thayer's index, No. 220. Also printed in (40, IV, p. 176).

EXAMPLE 72

"I make it like the poet makes an epigram," Beethoven once said with regard to his canons.[22] The *esprit* and humor of these musical epigrams have often been praised, so it is unnecessary to stress the point again. That they not only sparkle with gaiety but also reflect Beethoven's inexhaustible fantasy and mastery will be seen by the examples under discussion, which represent only a part of the collection—from a particular angle—and with no special emphasis laid on their musical value. The canons, although not limited to humorous texts, are only a small out-of-the-way province of Beethoven's creative work, but they are proofs and products of the Beethoven intellect. True, some are merely casual jottings, but others are carefully polished compositions, which should be available to the music lover in a complete and up-to-date collection, like the other Beethoven works. If the preceding discussion will serve as a stimulus and groundwork for such a collection, it will have fulfilled its mission.

III. ADDENDUM

The examination of the data on Beethoven's canons resulted in the temporary deletion of four titles, providing "research brought no new information to light on the subject." Meanwhile this has occurred in the case of one of

[22] See (47).

the questionable compositions. Under the title, "An Un-published Riddle Canon by Beethoven," in the *Neues Winterthurer Tagblatt* of May 21, 1949, Hess published a small facsimile of the canon *Da ist das Werk, sorgt um das Geld*,[23] with an accompanying article.

As already mentioned, Riemann (40, v, p. 408–409) and Frimmel (6) questioned the genuineness of the com-position which is supposed to have been sent to Holz to-gether with the new finale of the B flat major quartet (Op. 130). Frimmel knew only of the existence of a copy made by Holz[24] and of the whereabouts of this "not fully certi-fied copy." However, he mentioned a tradition cited by Riemann according to which the "staff and notes of this

[23] A reprint was called to my attention several months later by the New York Beethoven scholar, Mr. Donald MacArdle.

In the July 1953 issue of *Music & Letters* (p. 275), Otto E. Albrecht (in referring to Willy Hess's article on "Beethoven's Lost Composition" in the July, 1952 issue of that publication) states that "Mr. Hess need not have gone to the lengths he described to locate the 'lost' canon . . . . Attention was called to this interesting trifle in my article 'Adventures and Discoveries of a Manuscript Hunter' in the *Musical Quarterly* for October, 1945, pp. 492–503, where a complete facsimile was published. The translation of this article in *Musica*, Vol. II (1948), pp. 129–38, was accompanied by a transcription of the canon." In view of the conditions existing in Europe immediately after the war, it is comprehensible that the article in question did not come to Hess's attention. However, it is less excusable that the translation of this article in *Musica* escaped the notice of both Hess and myself, although I was already in America at that time. On the other hand it is regret-table that Albrecht did not establish his priority four years earlier, when Hess first reported his discovery, so as to avoid similar over-sights in the future.

[24] "The Heiligenstadt Beethoven collection is supposed to have acquired this manuscript from Karl Holz's son, and it is said to have been exhibited on the occasion of a concert which took place at Bösendorfer's. Riemann, who was unable to give any more definite information about it when the fifth volume of Thayer's Life of Beethoven was in preparation, doubted the existence of this canon, the more since Beethoven received for the new finale not 12 but 15 ducats." (Willy Hess in *Music & Letters*, July, 1952).

gay composition were by Beethoven, while the Master dictated the words to his friend."

As Hess himself stated, Max Unger drew his attention to the autograph of this canon (which is in the library of the Peabody Conservatory of Music at Baltimore). Hess then obtained permission to publish the facsimile on the basis of a photostat which had been placed at his disposal. Everything else can be found in Hess as well as Thayer, Frimmel, and Lenz (21, v, p. 219). Here we have only to state that the canon exists and is very probably genuine. The handwriting in the facsimile (so far as a layman can judge) is assuredly Beethoven's, and the whole—text as well as notes—is uniform and apparently written off at once. The script[25] is very clear, so that the composition can be easily read even in the reduced facsimile. It follows herewith.

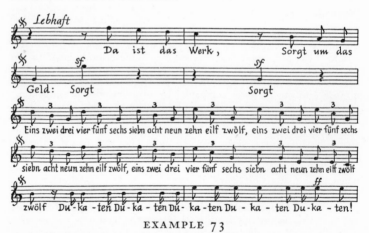

EXAMPLE 73

(Three commas and an exclamation point have been added.)

[25] The first eighth note of bar 2 could also be taken for *a*, but it is much more probable that it is *bb*. The text reads: "There is the work, see about the money, 1, 2, 3, 4, 5, 6, 7, 8, 9, 10, 11, 12 ducats."

CHAPTER IX

Why Did Beethoven Write the Fourth Overture to Fidelio?

I**N** an article on the "position of the great *Leonore* over-ture in *Fidelio*," which appeared in the *Allgemeine Musikzeitung* in 1936, Felix Weingartner entered a controversy which has raged in different stages and from various angles for well over a century. True, his remarks had reference only to a special case at that time—they criticized Mahler's practice of inserting *Leonore* No. 3 between the dungeon scene and the second finale. But they served at the same time to revive the whole hotly contested question bearing on the existence of four overtures to the opera.

If we consider Beethoven's own wishes in the matter, of which there is incontestable proof, then the principal question in the problem of the four overtures presented by Weingartner centers on only two of them, namely, the second of the two large ones in C major (*Leonore* No. 3) and the small one in E major (*Fidelio* overture). For Beethoven withdrew *Leonore* No. 1 and it was not used for the opera—in any case with his authorization. In the second version of the opera, however, *Leonore* No. 3 replaced *Leonore* No. 2. Though we of a later generation are capable of appreciating the greatness of *Leonore* No. 2 and would be as reluctant to part with it as with *Leonore* No. 3, the fact still remains that the composer himself withdrew *Leonore* No. 2 as an introduction to his opera in favor of the revised version known as *Leonore* No. 3.

The practice in *Fidelio* performances therefore alternates chiefly between the E major overture and *Leonore* No. 3. Opinion is unanimous that the fourth overture cannot compare with the third in spirituality and artistic content. But there is also a feeling that the gigantic structure of *Leonore* No. 3 (even as sound!) completely overpowers the first scenes of the opera—which furnish the setting for the superhuman figures and tremendous events that hold the stage later on. According to the subjective attitude of the conductor, one or the other overture is chosen to fulfill one or the other aesthetic demand—or both at once by trying repeatedly (at least since the time of Hans von Bülow) to find a place in the performance for both overtures. In all the arguments advanced by practicians, conductors, and writers on music to support their contrary points of view,[1] one misses, strange to say, a more serious examination of the very question that should really be the first and foremost one if the problem is to be removed from the sphere of the subjective; namely, the question if and how Beethoven himself reached a decision in the matter. There are naturally any number of persons who feel that he said his last word on the subject when he wrote the E major overture and that this should be recognized and accepted as the absolute expression of his will. However, so long as there is any uncertainty as

[1] Arthur Seidl's essay, *Leonore Fragen* (24), gives a well-oriented survey of the aesthetic arguments and practical experiments covering the period up to the first World War.

to his reasons and motive for writing a fourth overture, doubts whether his "last word" also represents his real artistic will cannot be excluded.

The customary and traditional opinion is that Beethoven, with the lighter overture of 1814, wanted to meet the public of his day halfway—that this overture represents a compromise between his genius and practical theatrical considerations at that time. Schumann probably gave crassest expression to this viewpoint in his *Meister Raros, Florestans und Eusebius Denk-und-Dicht Büchlein*, where, under the title of "The Leonore Overture," he wrote that "Beethoven is said to have wept over the almost complete fiasco of the first performance in Vienna —in similar circumstances Rossini would have laughed at most. Beethoven allowed himself to be persuaded to write the new overture in E major, which could just as well have been turned out by any other composer. Thou hast made a mistake—but thy tears were genuine."

Here Schumann's point of view even agrees with that of Anton Schindler, who asserts that Beethoven rejected *Leonore* No. 2 and *Leonore* No. 3 "owing to their technical difficulty for the orchestra," and *Leonore* No. 3 in addition because "it was too long a work for its purpose," summing up the matter by saying that "one really does not know what to make of the Master." And even Riemann (40, III, p. 875) found it necessary to pose the question: "Did Beethoven write the E major overture because the large C major one was a fiasco? Did he make a concession to theatrical conditions when, instead of a symphonic work in the grand manner, he gave the opera a simple overture of more ordinary cut, which imposed no high demands on the receptiveness of the public?" But Riemann unfortunately fails to answer the question in the course of his otherwise acceptable commentary on the work.

If we now attempt to answer a question that hitherto has always been passed over[2] or treated cursorily (i.e., why Beethoven really wrote his fourth overture to *Fidelio*), it will be necessary first of all to visualize the situation that gave rise to this composition.

The first revision of *Fidelio* was due to stress of outward circumstances. The fiasco of the first performance, which was followed by only two more, together with the urgings of trustworthy advisers who saw in the character and disposition of the work itself one reason for its failure, induced Beethoven to subject his score to a thorough revision. That he undertook "this operation" (as Jahn alleges in the preface of his piano reduction of the second version) against "his own conviction and inclinations" is not altogether correct. According to Stephen von Breuning, who made the necessary revisions in the text with Beethoven's concurrence, "Beethoven himself observed a few imperfections in the treatment of the text at the first performances." And the revision of the score, for which Beethoven took his time—Wilhelm Altmann expressly calls attention to this fact in his preface to the Eulenberg *Fidelio*—is something quite different from the concessions wrested from him at the famous December conference at Prince Lichnowsky's in 1805, which ended in his deleting several numbers in their entirey. And this new revision also did not consist "exclusively of cuts," as Erich Prieger asserts in his preface to the piano reduction of the

[2] Thus in one of the newer biographies (3) we read regarding the E major overture: "The new overture was probably written to add to the interest of a revival, but the plan came to nothing because Beethoven did not finish it in time. He probably felt no particular inner compulsion to the work."

original *Leonore*. The reference to the new trumpet fanfare would be sufficient evidence in itself that creative
fantasy went hand in hand with the fundamental work
of abridgment, to say nothing of the composition of
Leonore No. 3, which was carried out instead of the intended abridgment of *Leonore* No. 2. But the fact remains—and that is the vital consideration in this connection—that the first revision of *Fidelio* did not spring from
Beethoven's free initiative and was undertaken through
the "need for drastic abridgment" (Jahn).

The situation was entirely different with the second
revision (third version) in 1814. This time it was Beethoven himself who found a new revision necessary for the
suggested revival of his work and who, when his permission for the performance was requested, made this expressly contingent on numerous changes being made
beforehand. And even if we did not have this report of
his new librettist, G. F. Treitschke, and even if we did
not possess Beethoven's letter to this new literary colla-
borator in which he wrote: "As for the rest, the whole
matter of the opera is the most wearisome thing in the
world; and I am dissatisfied with most of it—and—there is
hardly a piece in it to which in my present state of dis-
satisfaction, I ought not here and there to have patched
on some satisfaction"—even without this evidence, a comparison of the final *Fidelio* with the first or second version
of *Leonore* would show us that this last revision, which
was carried out with the highest degree of artistic wisdom, was inspired by the composer's own independent
conviction. One follows this revision from number to
number with the greatest admiration, noting how, by
sacrificing many ideas of value in the earlier versions, it
aimed at heightening the theatrical effect and enhancing

the musical impressiveness at the same time, and how apparently insignificant retouchings were also designed to intensify the expression, to bring out the important points. From the infinitely loving and infinitely laborious work —"the opera will win me the martyr's crown"—arose the new overture.

The psychological suppositions also speak against the assumption that Beethoven—in the act of making his opera meet his own highest critical standards—made concessions to extra-artistic considerations in providing a new overture. But the circumstances connected with the *Fidelio* revival also gave no occasion for concessions of any kind. Beethoven was then at the zenith of his popularity. In fact it was the drawing power of his name that induced the stage managers of the Royal Opera to select *Fidelio* for the benefit performance accorded them. Consequently Beethoven had no need to renounce *Leonore* No. 3 (or *Leonore* No. 2 either, for that matter), and he most certainly would not have done so if he had found them otherwise suitable as an introduction to his revised opera. Even with a lack of understanding on the part of the public, this overture would have achieved at least a *succès d'estime* and in no circumstances would it have stood in the way of a complete success of the opera.

A dispassionate appraisal of the actual circumstances of the case in itself refutes an assumption that Beethoven's decision to provide a new overture for the 1814 *Fidelio* was motivated in any way by outward circumstances. What really impelled him to write the E major overture was a purely artistic consideration, which we discover the moment we open the original version of the opera. There we find as the opening number Marzelline's air while the duet between Marzelline and Jacquino holds second place.

The position of the two numbers was not reversed until the revised version of 1814, which resulted in the present order. But this rearrangement, a far from incisive measure at the first glance, was for Beethoven a compelling reason for making changes in the overture as well. For the A major duet with the initial motif a–$c^\sharp$–e–$f^\sharp$ would not have been compatible with the C major of the hitherto existing overtures. The new scenic disposition, which opened the action with the A major duet, made it impossible to begin the opera with a C major overture.

If Wilhelm Altmann, in his preface to the Eulenburg *Fidelio* score, asserts that "the new E major overture . . . agrees in tonality with the A major duet, which now opens the opera while the former C major overture was followed by Marzelline's C minor air," we go even further and conclude that the collision of tonalities, which would have arisen between the new opening number of the opera and the original overture, was the primary reason and at the same time the artistic compulsion for composing a new overture. Furthermore, this assumption finds incontestable confirmation in one of Beethoven's sketches of the 1814 version of *Fidelio* cited by Nottebohm.[3] Here, in company with sketches of the new conclusion of Florestan's air (*Ich seh' wie ein Engel*), there is a sketch of a projected E major revision of *Leonore* No. 1 (Op. 138): first of all, the main theme of the *allegro* transposed to E major with transition to the *Seitensatz* and a new progression[4] (also referring to a previous motif of the *Hauptsatz*). Then the theme of the introductory *andante con moto* transposed to E major. Variants and accompanying mem-

[3] *Beethoveniana.* xx (The Overture, Op. 138).
[4] A few bars are reminiscent of the *Fidelio* overture, another passage of an idea of the great *Leonore* overtures.

oranda show that he intended to rework the material. The project of revising the older composition was abandoned, but the idea of a new key for the overture, which manifested itself in this form for the first time, was retained and led to the conception of the E major overture as we know it.

Naturally we do not know why Beethoven again dropped the idea of revising *Leonore* No. 1, but we can imagine any number of reasons for it. In the first place it would be contrary to his feeling for the expressive character of the keys to write a work conceived in C major in any other key. Furthermore he might have feared that by reworking the material he threatened to throw the wonderful composition, as it then stood, in the shade (as he had done by substituting *Lenore* No. 3 for *Leonore* No. 2), instead of allowing it a place in the concert hall as an *"overture caracteristique."* And finally his fantasy, which apart from this was kept in prescribed grooves through the revision of the opera itself, urged him on to new free creation. It still seems as though he had struggled through to a satisfactory solution when, in writing to Treitschke of the progress of the work on *Fidelio,* he spoke of the new overture as "the easiest part of it since I can do it new right from the start."

Apart from the evidence that it was really the question of key that brought the plan of a new overture to a head, the foregoing sketch affords us further interesting information which justifies perhaps a brief digression. If Beethoven, after deciding upon a new key for the overture, still thought of incorporating *Leonore* No. 1 in the final version of his opera, this shows (as Marx puts it) that he recognized it as fundamentally "the right one for the work." For though there could be no question of

adapting the two great *Leonore* overtures to the new key
—which indeed is not open to discussion—the selection
of the only remaining one, the small *Leonore* No. 1, is
by no means to be considered a last resource or an evidence
that he was content with it. Beethoven would have much
preferred to have written it "new right from the start,"
as he ultimately did. If *Leonore* No. 1 is really the first
Fidelio overture in point of time, as it is now taken to be
—even though not yet with certainty—and if according to
Schindler's familiar account the work was really "found
wanting" and "withdrawn" after a rehearsal in the presence of invited advisers, Beethoven would have quashed
that erroneous judgment on the standpoint of 1814 and
rehabilitated in his own opinion the work rejected a decade before. At all events, we of a later generation should
be grateful to that Areopagus for its erroneous verdict.
For had it not been for this, the world would never have
had the twin wonders of the two great *Leonore* overtures.

Now how do these two works stand with relation to
the *Fidelio* of 1814? Here we must come back to the two
once more because just at that time—at least Schindler's
account gives this impression—the difference in character
of these two sister works and the greater suitability of the
one or the other as overture to the opera seems to have
been actively discussed in Beethoven's intimate circle.
And though Beethoven had actually decided—as already
noted—against *Leonore* No. 2 by writing *Leonore* No. 3,
it is possible after all that from the 1814 standpoint he
might have been amenable to the arguments of those who
called *Leonore* No. 2 "more characteristic as an opera
overture"; *Leonore* No. 3, on the contrary, a "concert
overture." This would be conceivable if he had had the
two great C major overtures to choose from at that time.

But we can be sure that he had already definitely rejected *Leonore* No. 2 or *Leonore* No. 3 before he drew the logical conclusions from the rearrangement of the first numbers of the opera. For if he had really wished to retain one of the great *Lenore* overtures as introduction for his opera, the problem of the key relationship between the overture and the first number would have been solved, not from the side of the overture, but from the opposite direction—in case the problem had ever actually arisen; that is, should he really have been willing in these circumstances to alter the arrangement of the opening scenes. But the fact that he did so, and perhaps even suggested the new arrangement himself—since it served to heighten the musical effect—is proof conclusive that the question of the overture was already a *cura posterior* and consequently no longer applicable to the two *Leonore* overtures.

This elimination of the grandiose tone poems from the plan of the new *Fidelio* (granting the untenability of any concession on Beethoven's part) is explained solely by his exceptional sense of responsibility towards his art, which, so far as his opera is concerned, amounted to truly heroic self-sacrifice. The German edition of Thayer's biography (40, III, p. 426) quotes a remark of the composer in 1823 which occurred in a discussion of the *Fidelio première* of 1814, to the effect that the new overture was not ready in time because of "obstacles which had presented themselves" and had to be replaced by another overture of Beethoven's. "The people applauded [he said] but I stood ashamed. *It did not belong to the rest.*" There indirectly, from Beethoven's own lips, we have the reason for his action in the matter of the overture. In characterizing (a full decade later) the new overture written for the revival as belonging to the "rest," he makes it clear that he composed it expressly because he did not feel that the earlier overtures now met this requirement. The great *Leonore* overtures only belonged to *Fidelio* as a "whole" as regards their origin, but no longer by nature and dimensions. Rooted in the intellectual soil of the *Leonore* drama, conceived during the creative process of the *Fidelio* music, *Leonore* No. 2, like its successor the grandiose *Leonore* No. 3, had outgrown its original mission as an organic part of the opera and had become a "whole"—an independent organism in itself. What today any halfway aesthetically schooled critic can deduce for himself, i.e., the disagreement between the outer and the spiritual proportions of the great C major overtures and the layout of the opera, rising from homely workaday scenes to heroic deeds, would that be impossible for Beethoven himself, the Master moulding his creations with the highest economic wisdom, when he looked back upon his lyrical work after the passage of years? For that is probably the thought behind Schindler's assertion (40, p. 218) that the composer, "to judge by various indications," also recognized himself that *Leonore* No. 3 was too long for an opera overture. Beethoven was naturally as little concerned with the "unusual length" to which the "experts" objected as with Schindler's debated choice between *Leonore* No. 2 and *Leonore* No. 3. He was moved by the consideration that either one of the two great C major overtures was prejudicial to the economy of the total structure of the opera. And his remarks on the subject were given only an incorrect and primitive interpretation by the informant who placed his own ideological construction on the "different indications" he observed.

If one understands what it means when the creator of

such an unprecedented work as *Leonore* No. 2 is so dissatisfied with it that he wishes to melt it down, so to speak, in order to use its material for a second, altered moulding of the same musical vision, there can be no doubt that in view of this sense of artistic responsibility, which is unique in the whole history of art, Beethoven was also capable of drawing the logical deductions and of sacrificing the two overtures altogether, i.e., of separating them from the opera when the interest of the latter seemed to demand it.[5] In fact, we find a parallel case in the history of Beethoven's work: the elimination of the Grand Fugue from the plan of the B flat major quartet, Op. 130. In both cases, tradition speaks thoughtlessly and unintelligently of a "concession" while in truth the Master himself, with the keenest artistic insight, had decided to replace compositions which had outgrown their intended role within the total art work with compositions smaller in content and form, but more compatible with the unity of the 'whole."

To recapitulate: At the final revision of *Fidelio*, Beethoven for reasons of economy dropped first of all the two great C major overtures. When the necessity of another key for the overture arose, the small *Leonore* No. 1, which was to replace them, still seemed to Beethoven to

---

[5] Although speaking neither for nor against our argument, for the sake of completeness we must call attention to a strange passage in an 1814 sketchbook cited by Nottebohm in his *Zweite Beethoveniana* (p. 297–98). This has reference to three excerpts from the great *Leonore* "written after the overture in E major was finished." One of these shows four bars of the *allegro* theme with the addition, "bassoons," and the other two the opening bars of the *adagio*, each one with a rhythmical variant of the entry on *g*. A renewed preoccupation with the great *Leonore*, which interested Beethoven quite apart from his *Fidelio* worries, naturally does not affect the validity of our argument, especially since the E major overture was already finished. And even if Beethoven thought of retouching it again, he at all events never carried out the project.

be worth revising. But the revision in E major was abandoned and led to the composition of a new overture drawing its inspiration from the character of this key.

Marx's opinion, which has been current until quite recently, that the E major overture bore no inner relationship[6] to the opera (22), was already invalidated by Riemann (40), so that here we can dispense with the experiment of "interpreting the contents" of the overture to prove its spiritual kinship with the opera. However, a sentence from Riemann's discussion of the E major overture is especially significant in the light of our presentation. "Who is not reminded of Leonore's great aria by the tonality and the soft entry of the horns in bar 5?"

If we realize that the C major of the three *Leonore* overtures serves not only to effect an easy, natural connection with Marzelline's C minor–C major aria, that it represents rather the "framework key" of the opera as a whole, common alike to the overture and the final chorus, then at the same time we must view the abandonment of the original tonality of the overture as the loss of a previous factor of unity. This loss, however, is compensated by a solution of the tonality question that is as novel as it is ingeniously simple: through the choice of E major which—solely in view of the duet following the overture —was the obvious but by no means the only possible choice. Instead of the ordinary key agreement between the introduction and final movement, this establishes the relationship between the overture and the spiritual core of the opera: the key reference to the only musical number in which the heroine, revealing her innermost

---

[6] "It is one of the most brilliant compositions, sparkling with talent and artistic skill. But it has nothing to do with *Leonore*." The same from Bekker (3): "Like the *Nameday* overture, the *Fidelio* overture has the general festal character of a concert overture."

thoughts, stands alone before the spectators of the dramatic action. So, from this point of view as well, the choice of the key is proof that in the new overture Beethoven also had the "whole" in mind.

If, after this, the E major overture can be interpreted —subjective assumptions aside—in the sense of the figure "Leonore" (as Marx did with *Leonore* No. 1), it is perhaps permissible to speak here of a purely musical analogy. In his characterization of the overture, Riemann stresses the fact that "while the three other overtures employ the wonderfully moving introductory motif of Florestan's aria and overtures No. 2 and No. 3 the fanfare that heralds the rescue as well, there is nothing in the E major overture that stems from the opera." Is not perhaps the brooding C major *pianissimo* that surges up to the great climax in the second *adagio* (from bar 7) a faint premonition of the passage: *"der* [Florestan] *kaum mehr lebt und wie ein Schatten schwebt"?* If so, then in this "unprogrammatic" overture the figure of Florestan would still be introduced indirectly, like an ominous shadow cast by coming events.

CHAPTER X

The Battle of Victoria

ONE would think that by this time Beethoven's entire creative work would be the intellectual property of the world of music. But this is not the case. There are a considerable number of compositions that are never played, or as good as never. It is a widespread belief among musicians and music lovers that when one knows the works that appear regularly on our concert programs, one knows the whole Beethoven. So it is generally assumed that the less familiar things, or those which have been entirely shoved into the discard, are of no importance, or even weak. Of course, there are a number of compositions, those dating from his very early youth or *pièces d'occasion*, written hastily and without interest, which from the purely artistic point of view no longer mean anything to us.[1] But these apart, there is still a sufficient amount of musically rewarding material among the un-

[1] Personally I feel that nothing of Beethoven's is lacking in interest, even if only as a contribution to our knowledge of his personality and development as an artist. It is also difficult to understand that only a part of the Conversation-books have been published as yet and that a large number are still awaiting examination and publication.

used stock to fill several chamber music, orchestral, and choral concerts as well as song recitals.[2]

How can we explain that? With the exception of works that are inappropriate in style for the concert hall, such as the canons for example, it is a question in part of works unsuited for ordinary concert performance owing to their scoring (chamber music for curious combinations, wind instrument ensembles, etc.) or of those which no longer have any message for us owing to a purely topical text. In addition, there are certain compositions which are outweighed by others of a similar category, and finally, those against which there is simply a traditional prejudice.

One work of this last group, which played a decisive role in Beethoven's life but has been simply jettisoned by later generations without considering it further, is the subject of this essay, the famous and discredited so-called Battle symphony, Op. 91, or as the complete title reads, *Wellington's Victory or the Battle of Victoria*.

We will first briefly run through the history of this extraordinary piece, which Thayer gives in detail. For it not only explains how the work came to be looked upon with contempt, but at the same time helps to remove existing prejudices by giving us the correct attitude towards a composition outside the general category of Beethoven's music.

The parent of the idea was Johann Nepomuk Maelzel whose friendly relations with Beethoven are recalled by

---

[2] And also an evening in the theater if—apart from the original *Leonore*—one thinks of the beautiful music to the *Ruins of Athens* and the final chorus *Zur Weihe des Hauses*, which was written later, to say nothing of a reconstruction of the choreography to the *Prometheus* ballet and a halfway practical text for the music to *King Stephan*.

the canon on the "great metronome" and *Banner der Zeit* (the Time-tamer). In the "Art Cabinet" that this "famous local citizen and court mechanician" exhibited to the Viennese in the winter of 1812–13, special interest was aroused by the Panharmonicon, a huge automaton instrument[3] for the mechanical production of military band music. Maelzel also intended to exhibit his mechanical player in London, and Beethoven (whose income was unfortunately reduced through the money depreciation following the wretched *Finanzpatent*) thought seriously of taking this opportunity to go to England with the inventor. He therefore was willing to write a work for the Panharmonicon, which already had works by Handel, Haydn, Cherubini, and Moscheles on the barrel, and fell in with Maelzel's astute suggestion to design the work to commemorate an event which was then the object of general rejoicing in Vienna—the great victory won by English troops under Wellington over the Napoleonic forces at Victoria, Spain, on June 21, 1813. And he also accepted Maelzel's suggestion to score the work for a real orchestra since a concert performance in Vienna promised to be a sufficient drawing card to finance the projected journey.

The *Battle of Victoria* was performed for the first time at a charity concert for the benefit of Austrian and Bavarian war invalids—that noteworthy concert of December 8, 1813, which also marked the first performance of the Seventh symphony. If the symphony in A received an enthusiastic reception even then, the Battle symphony, as Maelzel had foreseen, proved a sensation. The participating musicians under Beethoven's personal direction

[3] Riemann called it "Panharmonium"; Beethoven (in a letter) "Panharmonika."

were, as we know, all the local and visiting artists of distinction, from Salieri (the Court Conductor "who did not consider it beneath him to beat time for the drums and cannonades") to young Meyerbeer, who with Hummel served the "heavy guns"! From the chamber virtuosi Schuppenzigh (Beethoven's favorite violinist) and Spohr, to the traveling double-bass virtuoso Dragonetti. The success was so brilliant that after two "repeat performances," on December 12 and January 2, Beethoven was able to give two more during the course of the next three months. The Battle Symphony which (as he put it) "completely bowled over the Viennese" carried him to the pinnacle of popularity.

But voices gradually began to be heard that condemned the work as mediocre, some even going so far as to call it "unworthy of a Beethoven." And this verdict has become so firmly implanted in the consciousness of later generations that the work can be characterized as a forgotten or, more exactly, suppressed work.

It takes tremendous impertinence on the part of small-minded persons to defend Beethoven's artistic dignity from Beethoven himself. The motives back of the Master's acceptance of Maelzel's suggestion (the real reason was the pecuniary difficulties in which he found himself) required neither justification nor extenuation. The question remains: how did Beethoven carry out the assumed task from an artistic point of view?

Naturally the Battle Symphony cannot sustain comparison with Beethoven's symphonies. But such a comparison would be totally erroneous. Here his sole aim and purpose was to write one of those battle pieces played at the outdoor band concerts at the beginning of the twentieth century, which in Beethoven's time and even long before were equally popular with broad masses of the public. That a genius who had created the *Eroica* should find no inner compulsion to depict a realistic battle in music is as reasonable an assumption as that Beethoven (quite apart from his having to write it hastily) did not feel called upon to expend any great amount of brain work on such a primitive artistic project. It is significant enough that he took over from Maelzel not only the idea, but also the entire compositional plan of the battle music. He let Maelzel conceive and sketch in detail the drum marches and trumpet flourishes of the enemy armies and adopted his suggestions regarding the use of the English and French national anthems.[4]

And still Beethoven did not renounce his principles even in this occasional work, planned deliberately for its sensational and popular appeal. There is no doubt that he wanted to satisfy the demands of the average public for once; and he ventured into an ambit far removed from the sphere of Beethoven spirituality. But just because he correctly gauged the genre with which he had to do, he was able to turn out a work that was a brilliant example of its kind. The themes are not those suited to a symphony. But his ideas invariably strike the bull's-eye. Furthermore, he not only dedicated all his technical skill to it, but warmed up to the task and the sparks from the flint of his genius took fire. So without any violation of style he wrote in the Beethoven hand an unprecedented, and in its way unsurpassable, composition in the given genre. The *Battle of Victoria* is not a work "unworthy of a Beethoven," but a curiosity, and a curiosity at that which only a Beethoven could produce and which, if taken as it was intended to

---

[4] Some years before, in fact, Beethoven had written pianoforte variations on the themes of *God Save the King* and *Rule Britannia*.

be taken, would cause a furor even today. Some of the orchestral players are said to have looked on it as a "terrific" joke, and they were not entirely in the wrong. Here Beethoven undertook something that from the point of view of art was alien to his style. But he carried it off in his own distinct way—with his tongue in his cheek.

How highly he himself thought of it is shown by the detailed instructions and explanations for concert performance that he indicated in the score. These designate the number of instruments, the position of the different choirs, and the direction of the unusual apparatus. He specifies in detail the instruments for the percussion "battery" and how the "approach of the armies" is to be simulated realistically. Thus he demanded two complete and entirely independent wind choirs for the English and French armies, which combine during the further course of the work but must be maintained 'by all means" right up to the end—duly considering the dynamical requirements. "The rest of the orchestra must naturally be as strong as possible in proportion," and the "larger the hall, the more instruments there should be." He considered it very important not to substitute the normal Turkish drums ("the real Turkish drum does not belong in the orchestra") for the two large drums "which were to imitate the cannon." Here he expressly wished the large instruments used in theaters for "making thunder" ("five Viennese feet square"). These heavy guns, along with the rattles for imitating gunfire, and the fanfares and drum rolls (approaching from the distance) were to be located outside the orchestra at the farther end of the hall, out of sight of the audience. But with all his delight in this din and hubbub, he did not want the racket of the salvos to "darken" the orchestral music. Therefore the gunfire (except the final *presto* of the battle) should never begin at the opening of a new section. He wanted "the theme of each section" to be heard. Moreover, he himself marked the gunfire in the score, particularly the cannonades, using special indications for it. It is strange—one might almost say fantastic—to see large black and white circles above the staves of an ordinary orchestral score, to indicate the English and French cannonades!

Let us now try to describe the unusual score, as far as this is possible in mere words. First of all we hear a drum march which begins softly in the distance, and then increases to a *fortissimo* to symbolize the approach of the English army. An English military fanfare enters, followed by the English anthem, *Rule Brittania*, which, beginning softly, also gradually grows louder. This is scored in the manner of the military bands of that day and augmented later by the string choir. The same is repeated on the French side.[5] After a new drum march and fanfare, we hear the then popular French marching-song, *Marlborough s'en va-t-en guerre*. The French open the attack. A new trumpet call resounds as "challenge" from their positions which is returned by the enemy forces. And then the battle begins.

The movement is in three sections. First a motif flares

EXAMPLE 74

up which illustrates the discharge and whirring of a shell. Intensification (stepwise harmonic progressions and ex-

[5] Strange to say, both times the same except that the English is in E flat while the French is in C with the penultimate bar omitted.

plosive rhythms, recalling the thunderstorm of the *Pastorale* symphony) is effected at first by simple transposition, then after a few bars by thrilling diminution of the groups. A Beethoven storm bursts forth. This first section, which is naturally accompanied by the necessary cannonades, clatter of musketry, and trumpet calls, passes quickly into a *meno allegro.* Harking back to a French trumpet fanfare carried by *fortissimo* chords, the orchestra prepares the entry of a new motif:

EXAMPLE 75

which by means of inversion, syncopated counterpoint, etc., is developed to an effective battle picture, stalling finally in an organ point. And now the climax. Under the designation *Sturmmarsch* (assault) the seemingly simple theme of the *allegro assai,* which begins at this point, progresses by the very primitive compositional device of a stepwise ascent (cobbler's work!):

EXAMPLE 76

One must only imagine this theme in a unison of the deepest notes of the strings, accompanied by a thrilling drum rhythm and supported by more and more wind instruments; then one can readily picture the really stirring effect of this assault. Here in the deafening discharge of elementary rhythmical-dynamical forces we have a fore-taste of twentieth-century orchestral effects (Stravinsky, the Potemkin film). In addition, a continuously increasing pace leads to a *presto*. A trumpet call of the English merges into the familiar theme of *Rule Britannia,* which now amidst the swirling arabesques of the strings proceeds in *strettos* to a mighty climax. A fragment of the Marl-borough theme vainly tries to maintain itself (symbol and status of the battle), but it breaks up more and more, pulls itself together again, and finally succumbs in the sighing wind instruments. The *Marlborough* theme in minor mode and in funeral-march rhythm, fades away in a quivering tremolo of the strings, which characterizes the end of the battle. As a strategist also, Beethoven "goes the whole works," even to the knockout. The English guns thunder up to the last moment, after the French have long been silenced.

The Victory Symphony then follows, as part two. After a short *intrada,* thundered out by four trumpets over a drum bass, a stirring festal march begins which, rhythmically related to the second *Fidelio* finale, has something of the triumphant character of the final theme of the C minor symphony. Even though the movement may seem lighter in weight and more loosely put together than the corresponding thematic structures of Beethoven's greater works, there is no mistaking the claws of the lion. The superhuman shout of exaltation of the dominant seventh chord as it swings from the dominant of the domi-nant of the parallel key back to the main key[6]—the ecstatic gasps of the syncopated close—this could only have been

---

[6] Somewhat related to the wild outbreak in the *fortissimo* of the diminished seventh chord on the simultaneous words, "*befrei'n*," "*Rache*", and "*Wütrich*" in the quartet of the second act of *Fidelio.*

written by a Beethoven! The English national anthem (*piano*, carried by woodwinds) interrupts the march with a sudden change of harmony. The march resounds again and the national anthem is repeated, now more richly ornamented—interrupted by acclamations and a flourish of triumpets as it were—then, in a stirring development, to lead to the great final apotheosis after a highly original transition to a short but extremely artistic and ingenious fugato. Beethoven (as he expressed it) "wanted to show the English in a way what a blessing *God save the King* is!"

It goes without saying that the *Battle of Victoria*, in view of its genre and unusual scoring, can claim no permanent place in the repertory. But it is equally certain that it deserves to be known and for this reason should be played from time to time. This deliberate and intentional potboiler and thriller in its day (as its history shows) has been raised through Beethoven's fantasy far above all topical considerations and represents a curiosity which, taken as such, would "bring down the house" even today.

"But I've got you at last, you Beethoven devotees! I should like to rage against you quite differently and give each and every one of you a gentle cuff when, goggle-eyed, you begin to rave and say grandiloquently: 'Beethoven always sought only the grandiloquent; he flew from star to star, away from the earthy.' 'Today I'm really unbuttoned' was his favorite expression when he was in a jovial mood. And then he roared like a lion and banged about, for he was always unruly and tempestuous." These words from Schumann's discussion of the *Rage over the lost penny* can be applied *mutatis mutandis* to the condemned Battle Symphony and should be well *pondered* in this connection.

CHAPTER XI

Annotations on Some Pianoforte Sonatas

THE pianoforte sonatas Op. 2 and Op. 111 represent the corner and capstone of Beethoven's creation in the field of the pianoforte sonata. The sonata trilogy Op. 2 (published in 1796 and dedicated to Joseph Haydn) seems to have been known in Vienna in manuscript form as early as the spring of 1795. The C minor sonata, Op. 111, is dated January 13, 1822, and fell between the maturing of the *Missa Solemnis* and the gestation of the Ninth symphony. The C sharp minor sonata, Op. 27 (if we go by the symphonies) stems from the period between the first and second symphonies. And after the *Eroica*—in the *Fidelio* period—the *Appassionata* was conceived and carried out. Finally the composition of the C minor variations, issued without opus number, dates from the year 1806 when this great F minor sonata was completed.

The C minor variations, Op. 191, can be characterized as a grandiose "study." Naturally this word is not to be understood in the sense of dry brain work, but—like Chopin's perhaps most genial creations, the Etudes, or the superb Paganini Variations of Brahms—as studies in the sense of the systematic treatment of a particular artistic-technical problem. That in Beethoven's case such work lay in the creative sphere scarcely needs to be emphasized. The C minor variations are concerned with a dual problem: to exhaust all the arts of variation on a seemingly unpretentious theme, and at the same time to utilize all the myriad possibilities of the pianoforte, technical as well as tonal. The way Beethoven has conjured an unheard-of richness of changing figures out of the brief and apparently barren theme by blending the old *chaconne* technique with the modern type of variations makes this cycle of variations one of the most ingenious works in the whole field of pianoforte literature. The development of large forms from the eight-bar theme is characteristic of Beethoven's mode of thought and compositional methods in broad dimensions. Not that the original structure has been altered. On the contrary, several related variations are always grouped together, two or three at a time, to form larger groups, associated one with the other partly through motivic logic, partly through contrast. And over and above this, the whole unites to form one great trilogy: two sections in the minor mode separated by a middle section in the major.

The tremendous energies and stresses that charged Beethoven while wrestling with the Mass and the Ninth symphony also come out in the C minor sonata, Op. 111. The work has only two movements. Here everything demanding expression is concentrated to the utmost, compressed into the briefest space. Titanic forces roll up in the introductory *maestoso*, are released in the main theme of the first movement now firmly established after three entries, then to rush forward irresistibly, intensified still more through a stanching of the motion. The serene, inward second theme is hardly a contrast—merely a pause, a confirmation. Here not the second theme but the second movement forms the actual contrast. (In this respect Beethoven's last sonata presents still another new solution of the sonata problem!) The rapture of the blissful *arietta* is the direct opposite of the electric storm of the *allegro* and at the same time the goal of the *allegro*—fulfillment after Faustian struggle. Therefore in this sonata the *adagio must* remain the last movement.

How can one describe this *adagio* in words? A divinely inspired theme and variations such as only Beethoven, the "last Beethoven," could write. From rapture to transport, from the ecstasy of "I will not let thee go except thou bless me" to transfiguration in unearthly bliss.

The A major sonata, the second of the three early works of the great master of the pianoforte sonata that were published simultaneously, sprang from the joy of life, the sheer love of playing. Gaiety paired with energy characterizes the first movement; grace and power join hands in the final *rondo*. But there is also a gentle touch of melancholy even in the first movement. A Beethoven abyss yawns before us in the development section. And in the wonderful *largo appassionata*, the longing of the young Beethoven pours forth in a soul-stirring song, heightened to the point of tragedy.

The tragedy of the young Beethoven: the C sharp minor sonata, Op. 27, No. 2. A sentimental urge for interpretation has given the work the cheap byname of "Moonlight sonata." He who invokes the moon here will see threatening cloud masses rolling up even in the first movement, with storm-driven fragments racing across it in the tempest of the finale. But scenery is not necessary. The *adagio*, which opens this *Sonata quasi una fantasia*, is melancholy, a lament, a restrained sigh transmuted into music. The finale—a song of despair—an elementary outbreak of irrepressible passions. The delicate lights of the *allegretto* falling in between merely deepen the dark shadows of the framing movements. Beethoven dedicated the work to his pupil, Countess Giulietta Guicciardi, whom many scholars believe to be the mysterious "Immortal Beloved." We do not require such knowledge to understand the language of this tone poem.

The F minor sonata, Op. 57, is also a tragedy in music. This too has received the byname *Appassionata*, but not from Beethoven himself. If the idea of the sonata form can be characterized as a contrast between two themes, then the first movement of this sonata represents one of the finest and most profound realizations of this idea. Contrast of two themes; conflict of two themes; fight to the finish—that, from the purely musical angle, is the content of this tremendous movement. The two themes spring from one single root: the gigantic, somber, main theme, pregnant with explosive material, the *pianissimo* of which represents the intense hush beforre the tornado. And the noble *cantilena* of the song theme, which vainly tries to carry the major key against the dominating minor, but finally goes down in the battle, sucked into the ambit of the minor and swallowed up by the daemonic main theme. In the D flat major *andante*, the music pauses to take breath, to comfort, arouse new hope. But all in vain. Destiny is fulfilled in the uncanny nocturne of the breathlessly rushing finale, from which the major key is permanently banned. Nothing but wails and moans from the infernal regions.

CHAPTER XII

"The Upper Pitches of the Voices More Through the Instruments"
"Die Höhe der Stimmen mehr durch Instrumente"

ONE of Beethoven's various memoranda found among the sketches of the finale of the Ninth symphony and communicated by Nottebohm in his *Zweite Beethoveniana* (p. 186) reads: "The upper pitches of the voices more through the instruments." According to Nottebohm, this annotation "made while at work on the final chorus, means that the upper pitches of the voices should be supported by the instruments." "If this interpretation is correct [he goes on to say], it would prove that Beethoven was conscious of the reproof frequently brought against him that he disregarded the compass of the voices—that he wrote the vocal parts too high."

Nottebohm's interpretation does not seem to get the point of the words in question. The first objection would be that instrumental support would in no way facilitate matters for singers confronted with an uncomfortable *tessitura*. At most it would hide unevennesses in performance. Furthermore, we find that in the finale of the Ninth symphony, at all events, the idea is not applied in the sense of Nottebohm's interpretation. The solo voices are without instrumental support and are just as exposed as ever, and the orchestral support of the chorus—if one can ever think of the orchestra part as supporting the choral part of a symphony—nowhere indicates that any special consideration was paid to the high pitches of the voices. Therefore another interpretation must be found for Beethoven's aphorism.

The following illustration of one of Beethoven's compositional procedures furnishes one solution. In the original version of *Fidelio*,[1] Leonore sings:

O na-men, na-menlo-se Freude

EXAMPLE 77

In the final version we find:

O na-men, na-menlo-se Freude

EXAMPLE 78

Thus the original melody is retained, but in view of the uncomfortable *tessitura* it has been allocated in part to the instruments. The upper pitches of the human voice are *replaced* "by instruments." This also improves the declamation since it does away with the stress on the unaccented syllable "lose."

The *Missa Solemnis* provides another illustration. At the end of the first section of the *Gloria*, the sopranos rise to a high *a* (in three octave unison with the other voices), and floating above this sustained high note, the string choir, playing in unison, carries the melodic line an octave higher as though it were infinite.

[1] Piano arrangement of *Leonore* by Erich Prieger.

EXAMPLE 79

At this overpowering climax, which once heard can never be forgotten, the instruments carry the vocal melodic line to pitches beyond the compass of the human voice. The upper pitches of the voices are *supplemented* by the instruments.[2]

It is obvious that Beethoven had such a procedure in mind when he wrote the words: "The upper pitches of the voices more through the instruments." But since he was unable to express the idea in one succinct formula—perhaps the two verbs "replace" and "supplement" also do not yet cover all the given possibilities—he chose a catchphrase serving merely as a personal reminder for himself alone.[3]

The fact that this interpretation finds as little support in the finale of the Ninth symphony as does Nottebohm's does not nullify it. Such a memorandum naturally does not need to signify a new idea that has occurred to him or a guiding principle for the future. For some reason Beethoven might have committed to writing a long-estab-

[2] Similar procedure at *omnipotens* and *et ascendit.*

[3] One might perhaps cite cases falling in the province of tone color—substituting "brightness" for the upper pitches by having the instruments play an octave higher than the voices (e.g., in the *Missa Solemnis*, the progression of the violins in the *Laudamus Te* following the first *Glorificamus Te* of the soprano.

lished principle or have recalled this principle to mind when a corresponding problem arose again.

It is unnecessary to point out that the purpose of this observation is not so much to comment on a casual monolog of Beethoven as to draw attention to a peculiar stylistic device which seems to be intimated by this annotation and the ingeniousness of which is still little appreciated.

CHAPTER XIII

Non si fa una cadenza

A RE we really insensitive to this question, or are there weightier reasons for it? An eminent violinist plays the Beethoven concerto and—technical proficiency apart —plays with all the abandon and expression of one who knows and feels what he is playing; in short, one cannot imagine anything more beautiful. Then suddenly—the fatal six-four chord! the inevitable cadenza! And instead of Beethoven we hear the famous virtuoso X. Instead of music bringing us inward joy, we are amazed at a "record" technical exhibition (even though the cadenza be by Joachim or Kreisler)—that is, if we do not try to close our ears to it until Beethoven returns again with the liberating trill.

This requires no long aesthetic demonstration. One need only have ears capable of grasping music. Who in listening to the Beethoven violin concerto does not feel himself suddenly brought down to earth by the cadenza? But anyone—mental reservations and "reasons" aside— who cannot confess to such a feeling has never fully followed Beethoven in his lofty flight. The same thing is true—to cite a crass example—of the first movement of Beethoven's G major pianoforte concerto. But—argue the wiseacres—"a concerto is a virtuoso composition! The cadenza is a traditional part of it! Beethoven himself . . ." The objections are too well known, too founded on good faith and too convincing for them to be passed over without serious examination.

Render unto the virtuoso that which is his. To decry virtuosity as such simply because in certain circumstances it conflicts with higher artistic interests, or to inveigh against it as a principle foreign to art is not only pedantic but also the proof of positive ignorance. The concerto has arisen from the needs and for the needs of virtuosity (certainly not to the detriment of art) as a type of composition "which is intended to display the performer's virtuosity" (34). Whoever writes concertos—up to now or in the future—will try to understand this intention and do justice to it. Beethoven also wrote his concertos (and other works) for "virtuoso" ends, and as far as technique is concerned, took these ends fully into account. But for such purposes and objects (here Beethoven could not help being Beethoven) works arose in which the virtuoso aspect was certainly not neglected, but so applied to higher aims (artistic content, idea, inspiration, or whatever one may choose to call it) that instead of being the goal, it seems to have become the major premise.[1] Beethoven's concertos differ to this extent from others of the same category which, to judge by their outstanding characteristic, we are accustomed to call "virtuoso" concertos (in the sense of having less artistic value). Beethoven's

---

[1] "It is the composer's secret task [wrote Marx in his still readable Beethoven biography] to overcome the "difficulty" of the concerto-form in the form itself through the importance of the content. The difficulty is that the task—to treat one instrument and its performance as the main issue and the incomparably richer and more important orchestra as a mere auxiliary—is really an artistic anomaly."

concertos, along with a number of similar works by other masters, are just as much or just as little "virtuoso pieces" as Chopin's etudes perhaps—without prejudice to their pedagogic value—are technical exercises. In them we possess art works which we love and listen to for their own sake, and not because of the virtuoso who plays them. On the other hand, we well know that it takes a virtuoso to interpret such art works to perfection. Therefore we are grateful to him and acclaim him for it. And so the virtuoso profits by it. If he is not content with mastering the technical difficulties presented by the work, then he is free to play something else. But he does not tear a homogeneous art work to pieces by interpolations (cadenzas!) intended to display his maximum technical accomplishments, nor does he distort a text, the poetic beauty of which is sacred to us, by parenthetical remarks no matter how clever or amusing they may be.

However, it is quite true that the cadenza is traditional. "Shortly before the end of the first movement (wrote Riemann), and often of the last as well, a *fermata* over the six-four chord usually affords opportunity for the insertion of a free fantasy on the main theme." But a tradition alone is not sufficient to justify something which cannot be vindicated on other counts.

But did not Beethoven himself write the six-four chord in question at the designated point? And did he not expressly add the direction: "Cadenza"? He would certainly never have hesitated to break with a custom of which he disapproved. Shall we out-Herod Herod?

Let us picture to ourselves the situation when Beethoven brought out his first pianoforte concertos. Composer and virtuoso in one, he whose gift of improvisation was the wonder and admiration of his contemporaries, certainly had no call to oppose a practice which "afforded an opportunity to interpolate a free fantasy in a legitimately artistic form." The cadenzas were *free fantasies* which were intended to show off the player's virtuosity and talent for improvisation in the most brilliant manner. Who would not have heard such cadenzas from a Beethoven!

We learn furthermore that in 1804 he took a cadenza for granted even when his concertos were played by others. The incident recounted by his pupil Ferdinand Ries also dates from this period.[2] Ries was to make his first public appearance with the C minor concerto and asked his Master to write a cadenza for him.

But Beethoven "refused and told me to write one myself and he would correct it." It was characteristic of Beethoven's attitude at that time that he not only permitted foreign matter to be inserted in his works, but actually ordered it. In any case, this time he supervised the procedure and could prevent slips of taste, and so on. We also see from Ries's account that Beethoven did not grudge him his triumph as a virtuoso.

"Beethoven was very satisfied with my composition [he continued] and made few changes; but there was one extremely brilliant and very difficult passage in it, which, though he liked it, seemed to him too venturesome; wherefore he told me to write another in its place. A week before the concert he wanted to hear the cadenza again. I played it and floundered in the passage. He again—and this time a little illnaturedly—told me to change it. I did so, but the new passage did not satisfy me. . . . At the public concert, Beethoven (who conducted) sat down quiet-

[2] Wegeler and Ries. "*Biographische Notizen über L. van Beethoven,*" quoted from 16, 1, p. 93–94.

ly. I could not bring myself to play the easier one. When I now boldly began the more difficult one, Beethoven violently jerked his chair, but the cadenza went through all right and Beethoven was so delighted that he shouted 'Bravo' loudly. This electrified the entire audience and at once gave me a standing among the artists."[3]

Mozart proceeded differently. He wrote cadenzas for his pupils when they played his pianoforte concertos in concert—and he well knew why.[4] But in the course of time Beethoven, whose creative work in the realm of the concerto (exclusive of the youthful work of 1784) covered a period of a good decade and a half, had evidently changed his original point of view. Otherwise—apart from his cadenza to the first and third movements of Mozart's D minor concerto—why did he write a series of cadenzas for his own concertos? He no more needed a written cadenza for himself than did Mozart. Did it please him, perhaps, to write down his own improvisations later? (His cadenzas to Mozart's D minor concerto give plausibility to the idea.) Or were these cadenzas new compositions? This would all amount to the same thing: the transitory, the improvised, was replaced by the permanent, the *res facta*. Hence Riemann asserted that "Beethoven also preferred to dictate to the virtuoso what he was to play at this point." In other words, by writing out his own cadenzas to his concertos, he could only have intended to keep others from adding free fantasies to his works.

We have Beethoven's own cadenzas for the four

[3] See also Bridgetower's account of Beethoven's delight over a virtuoso improvisation of the violinist in the Kreutzer Sonata. (40, II, p. 396).

[4] "Mozart wrote a large number of cadenzas for his pupils (K.V. 624, p. XXII, 18) which in all probability were cut to the measure of each individual's ability" (1, II, p. 240).

pianoforte concertos that precede the E flat major concerto as well as for the revision of the violin concerto as a
piano concerto.[5] And also for the G major concerto. The
last movement of this bears the annotation: *La cadenza
sia corta*. It should be short if it could not be dispensed
with entirely.[6] Is it due to chance or an oversight that the
direction "cadenza," which is found in four of the pianoforte concertos and the last movement of the violin concerto, is missing in the first movement of the violin concerto at the point in question?[7] Beethoven was extremely
meticulous about his expression marks and directions for
performance. It looks as though the author of the violin
concerto, contrary to a manifest custom, could no longer
bring himself to endorse the insertion of a cadenza in the
first movement—in such a movement! With all sympathy
for the virtuoso's requirements—let him enjoy himself in
the last movement if it cannot be helped! *Cadenza ad lib.*
is written above the six wonderful little notes at the end
of the *larghetto*.

Thus Beethoven's written cadenzas represent a step
forward along the road leading imperceptibly to the
abolishment of the cadenza.[8] He took the final step in the
E flat major concerto. At the decisive point in the first

[5] Besides the cadenzas contained in the Complete Collection, there
are some more unpublished ones listed by Max Unger in his Catalogue
of the Bodmer Beethoven Collection in Zürich, Switzerland.

[6] See Abert's reference (1) to the shortness of the Mozart cadenzas
(also to Beethoven's short cadenza to Mozart's D minor concerto) and
the aberration of the "virtuoso period at the beginning of the 19th
century of developing the cadenzas to exhibitions of mere technical
virtuosity."

[7] Reference here is to the Peters Edition of the score.

[8] In the aforementioned catalogue Unger gives the date of composition for all the cadenzas listed therein—presumably 1809. The
cadenza to the C minor concerto and the Mozart D minor concerto
are lacking in the Collection. Unger very kindly explained the dating

movement we find the words at the heading of this essay
—the terse phrase: *Non si fa una cadenza, ma s'attacca
subito il seguente.* There should be no cadenza! An express prohibition. Does this prohibition refer *only* to the
E flat major concerto? Is this an isolated case? Or is it not
rather the result of a logical development, which, once
established (and definitely established in this instance),
is to be the general rule from now on? In Beethoven's
sense the interpretation would perhaps be: in Beethoven
concertos no cadenzas but his own. The same should be
true for the Mozart concertos with the exception of the
congenial Beethoven cadenzas to the D minor concerto.

The art of improvisation is no longer practiced nowa-
days; therefore the particular soil that gave birth to the
cadenza is lacking. Tradition has been unable to maintain
the vital element of the cadenza. It has preserved only the
dead form as an excuse for indulging in technical tours de
force. From this point of view likewise, the existing practice of grafting strange bodies on classical works is artistically untenable.

If the demand is accordingly made that only the cadenzas of the great masters be used in their concertos, then
in the case of works for which no cadenzas have been
provided, the question arises how the break—which is

to me in a personal letter as follows: "I believe they were all written
at approximately the same time, with the possible exception of those
for the Mozart concerto. Those to the C major concerto could also
not have been written before 1808 owing to the change in the compass
of the pianoforte. Nothing positive is known regarding Beethoven's
motive for writing them out. It is possible that they were written at
that time, since in March and April Beethoven was in no proper mood
for writing a big work of his own, owing to the arrival of the French
(which is why he restricted himself to excerpts from theoretical works
for the instruction of Archduke Rudolph)." And in line with the same
reasoning: "Perhaps he also thought of writing his own cadenzas since
he wrote them in at once in the last concerto."

nearly always noticeable—is to be filled in. One generally valid rule is naturally impossible. Each case must be decided individually as to whether or no a "filler" is actually necessary, and how best it is to be carried out. But from the viewpoint of form—one should not have the feeling that something is lacking nor should one note the hand of an outsider—this problem does not seem too difficult of solution—an unpretentious running passage, a simple trill or chain of trills, in certain circumstances two or three connecting notes[9] would be quite sufficient to join without a gap the *fermata*-crowned six-four chord with its natural harmonic resolution, the dominant.

But there is still another consideration which should not be passed over in silence for the sake of the present point of view. Since the cadenza is prescribed in the classical concerto and has therefore been carefully prepared, its omission might leave the impression of a "cause without effect" so to speak—to reverse a Wagner dictum. This would undoubtedly be a far lesser evil, as compared with the extraneous cadenza. But anyone wishing to avoid it nonetheless,[10] and desiring to have recourse to a cadenza, should at least be governed by Beethoven's other law: *La cadenza sia corta*. In the last analysis, everything rests with the player's sense of responsibility towards the art work.

[9] In the first movement of the Beethoven violin concerto, the two notes *g*, *f♯* are sufficient to join the *fermata a* with the trill on *e*. The cadenza in the first movement of the G major pianoforte concerto can be dispensed with in a similar way in case the player feels that Beethoven himself, in his cadenza to this movement (unlike that in the last movement) did not quite get back into the atmosphere of the work.

[10] Busoni found a happy solution of the cadenza problem in the violin concerto of Brahms—a cadenza at all events, but of such a nature that no one unfamiliar with the work would ever recognize it as such, or notice any gap. Perhaps the use of the kettledrum owes its inspiration to Beethoven's cadenza in the piano arrangement of the violin concerto. But such solutions are exceptions to the rule. They are only successful in the case of the elect and cannot with impunity be recommended for imitation.

CHAPTER XIV

Fidelio: An Ethical Confession

Although part of the permanent repertory, Beethoven's *Fidelio* occupies a peculiar place in opera literature. To us it represents not only a peak achievement in the field of music drama, but also a glorification in music of imperishable ethical ideas—an affirmation of the highest ideals of the human race.

It was due neither to a voluntary renunciation on the composer's part nor to the accidents of outward circumstance that *Fidelio* remained the only operatic work of the greatest dramatist of instrumental music. Beethoven was preoccupied more or less seriously with opera projects up to the end of his life. Yet only this once was it given him to find a material that—besides its essential dramatic fitness—fulfilled all his special demands for an opera libretto.

But as far as character goes, the *Fidelio* libretto, which as we know was founded on fact, does not represent an isolated case. On the contrary, it belongs to a type of material which was popular at the turn of the eighteenth century and figures in the history of music under the heading of "horror" or "rescue" opera.[1] The original

[1] That is, melodramatic material characterized by sensational incident and violent appeal to the emotions, but with a happy ending.

French text on which the opera was based had already been set to music by Gaveaux several years before and also by Paer in an Italian translation just previous to, or during, the time that Beethoven was working on *Fidelio*. After the Dresden *première* of Paer's opera *Leonora ossia l'amore conjugale* (Leonore, or Wedded Love), Beethoven to his great annoyance naturally had to select another title for his work, which came out later and was to have been called *Leonore*.

Unexpected rescue from death is unquestionably an effective theme for a drama. And at the proper point (the quartet of the second act: *Er sterbe, doch erst soll er wissen*) Beethoven developed it to a scene which for sheer dramatic impact and breathtaking suspense has no peer in the entire literature of music drama. But this scene alone, which it is true represents the climax and turning point of the action, could not have been the deciding factor in the choice of the text. For certainly a mind like Beethoven's could not have been interested in the portrayal of horrors with a happy ending in the sense of poetic justice just for the sake of the dramatic suspense. What really attracted him to the libretto and made him overlook the much-discussed dramatic weaknesses of the first version, which as we know underwent two revisions, was the inner content of the drama, which corresponded to his own deepest nature. He saw in it the reflection of an idea that he had nurtured in his heart all his life long and to which—after *Fidelio*—he as symphonist was to give artistic expression in two of his most grandiose creations, the Fifth and Ninth symphonies; an idea that we usually formulate as "through darkness to light," or which might also be expressed in his own words: "through suffering to joy."

"O Providence, let me sometime have one day of perfect happiness!" he wrote in 1802 in the deeply moving *Heiligenstädter Testament.* And in a letter in 1815: "We mortals with the immortal spirit are only born to joy and suffering, and one might almost say that the Elect receive joy through suffering." In this sense the dramatic action of *Fidelio* took on for Beethoven a personal-programmatic, and at the same time universal, significance. And viewed in this light, we can understand why the second finale had to undergo such a tremendous development after the real action was already over. The broad treatment of the *Hymn of Joy* is also conditioned by artistic-economic considerations through the necessity of balancing off the heavily charged atmosphere, and anyone who is tempted to condemn it as a lapse into the cantatalike has failed to grasp what Beethoven had at stake here. The second *Fidelio* finale, which plays the same role with respect to the whole as the final movements of the Fifth and Ninth symphonies, does not represent the end of an opera according to the stereotyped pattern, but it is the actual goal of the drama's development.

However, the text also offered further and more definite points of contact with Beethoven's philosophy of life and conception of the world, and his inmost personal experiences. What brings about the change in the action? "There is a Providence!" whispered Leonore to her husband before the decisive struggle. And Providence really does enter at the crucial moment. Writers on musical aesthetics have likened the Minister's entry to the introduction of the famous *deus ex machina*, which in antique drama and in opera up to the time of Gluck, was called upon to untie man's inextricable knots. It is true that the Minister appears by chance just at the right moment (and even a *deus ex machina* disguised as Providence would also be no real dramatic factor), but the Heaven-sent savior merely completes the work which was begun by Leonore through her own strength alone and which she would also have brought to culmination even without this miraculous intervention. After the foregoing development, we never for a moment doubt that she would be capable of carrying out her threat and killing the mortal enemy in order to save her husband. Providence is not introduced here because the librettist was faced with a dramatic dilemma, but in the Goethian sense of

> *Allen Gewalten zum Trotz sich erhalten*
> *Nimmer sich beugen,*
> *kräftig sich zeigen,*
> *rufet die Arme der Götter herbei.*[2]

Therefore Leonore—with all her confidence in help from on high—embodies Beethoven's own heroic ethics: "I will seize Fate by the throat." But this womanly figure must also have appealed to him in other ways than as a heroine. The opera was first produced under the title *Fidelio, or Wedded Love* and is still known today as the "Song of Songs of wedded love." "Love only—yes—this alone can give thee a happy life!" he wrote on another occasion. "O God, let me find her at last, she who will strengthen me in virtue, who is destined to be mine!" To him on whom Fate (the daemon of his genius and the misfortune of his deafness) had imposed the life of a solitary, Leonore became the symbol of an ideal wife, of the ethical principle of marriage. "Let him who has attained

[2] To stand firm despite all violence, never to give in, to be strong—calls forth the aid of the gods.

such a wife join in our joyful song." Beethoven glorifies
the happiness of wedded love in almost the same words as
he did many years later[3] in the finale of the Ninth symphony. And even before she recognized her husband in
the suffering figure in the dungeon, Leonore by her oath:
"Whoever thou art, I will save thee!" had transmuted
wedded love into the all-embracing love of mankind—into
humanity.

He who inspired Leonore's heroic love must also have
awakened Beethoven's humanity and deep compassion
over and above the appeal to his creative imagination. For
Florestan, the victim of cruel despotism, whose lament,
*In des Lebens Frühlingstagen ist das Glück von mir
geflohn* (Happiness fled from me in the springtime of
life), might well have touched the chord of Beethoven's
own sorrow, and whose patient endurance also recalls the
composer's mood at the time of the *Heiligenstädter Testament*, is not only an object of "tragic interest," he is the
very personification of violated human rights. Furthermore, "the noble person who contended for truth" and
now lies in fetters for his pains is the martyred champion
of an ethical ideal. One can, without hesitation, substitute
"right" for "truth" in the given connection and in so doing actually have "human rights" in mind.[4] We know

[3] We even find the identical text in the original version: "*Wer ein
holdes Weib errungen.*" *Leonore*, piano arrangement by Erich Prieger.

[4] There can be no doubt that Florestan, whom the Minister ad-
dressed as friend and the champion of truth, is a political fighter. When
in Pizarro's case "he ventured to uncover a crime," no paltry rascality
was meant such as a "corruption scandal" and the like, for otherwise
the words, "I made bold to speak the truth," would smack too much
of pathos. Pizarro must have been finally convicted for an analogous
or the same crime—the misuse of executive power to put the trouble-
some out of the way. From the action taken against a transgressor of
Pizarro's stamp (an individual case unknown to the Minister), we can
easily see the nature of the whole struggle waged by Florestan for
the cause of truth.

what human rights signified for Beethoven by his out-
burst at the news of Napoleon's coronation as emperor (as
related by his pupil Ries) which caused him to tear up the
title page of the *Eroica* with its dedication to Bonaparte.
"He's nothing but an ordinary mortal! Now he'll trample
all human rights in the dust ... become a tyrant!"

Thus the saving of Florestan's life, the undertide of
the dramatic action, became at the same time an artistic
confession of faith in the ultimate victory of justice and
the triumph of human love. For the figure of the Minister,
whose intervention finally crowns Leonore's work, simply embodies the idea of humanity. At this fateful turn of
events brought about "by justice linked with mercy," the
question is no longer one of Florestan and Leonore. Their
individual destinies merge into the collective and are raised
to a symbol of the fate of mankind. "O God, Thou lookest
into my inmost soul [we read in the *Heiligenstädter Testament*], Thou knowest it and understandest that love of
humanity and a desire to do good dwell therein." Beethoven, who in the finale of the first act expresses the suffering and hope of the nameless prisoners with the same sym-
pathetic fervor as he does the soul turmoil of the heroes
of his opera, expands in the finale of the second act the
"Song of Songs of wedded love" to the "Song of Songs of
the love of mankind." This is brought out even more
clearly in the quietly moving episode, which a phrase in
the Minister's speech ("Brother seeks brother, and when
he can help, he does so gladly") raises to tremendous significance, than in the exultant opening chorus of the folk
and the prisoners. These wonderful bars overflowing with
purest good will deserve the name *"Humanitätsmelodie"*
no less than the inspired *sostenuto assai* ("O God what a
moment!") which was taken from the cantata on the death

of Joseph II and, in the words of Riezler, "has been fitting-ly called the melody of humanity."

But the besmirched human dignity of the oppressed is restored by the glorified message of the brotherhood of man: the same spirit that imbued Beethoven's words to the "Immortal Beloved" when he wrote, "Man's humility before men pains me." The Minister turns to the prison-ers: "Kneel no longer slavishly before me. The severity of the tyrant is foreign to me!" Given the actual theme of the opera, it is unnecessary to point out that the entire action is permeated by the ideal of freedom, which is in-voked by the prisoners in hopeful yearning and by Flores-tan in transports of ecstasy. It is the same idea that Bee-thoven refound and glorified in *Egmont*.

The heroism of love and the heroism of moral convic-tion—optimism in deed and faith in divine and human jus-tice and goodness—these were the ideas that Beethoven deduced from his libretto and through the might of his genius and the ethos of his personality formed and fash-ioned to an art work and profession of faith. His ethical creed also comes out distinctly, conclusively, and up-liftingly in his instrumental works. But there it is less easy to define and demonstrate than in the opera where it has the assistance of the text. Therefore his ethics and philo-sophy of life come out more comprehensibly in *Fidelio* than in any of his works. And it is in this sense that Walter Riezler's words are to be taken: "Never did Beethoven reveal his soul as here."

Bibliography

1. Abert, Hermann. *Mozart*, 1920–21.
2. Altmann, Wilhelm. Article in *Allgemeine Musikzeitung*, No. 20, 1936, p. 20.
3. Bekker, Paul. *Beethoven.* 1911. (English translation by M. M. Bozman) London, 1925.
4. Blessinger, Karl. *Grundzüge der musikalischen Formenlehre.* Stuttgart, 1926.
5. Braunstein, Josef. *Beethovens Leonore-Overtüren.* Leipzig, 1927.
6. Frimmel, Theodore. *Beethoven Handbuch.* Leipzig, 1926.
7. —— *Canones. Beethoven Handbuch*, Vol. I.
8. Graf, Max. *Die innere Werkstatt des Musikers.* Stuttgart, 1910.
9. Heuss, Alfred. *Beethoven. Ein Charakteristik.* Leipzig, 1921. Second ed. Braunschweig, 1933.
10. Hess, Willy. "Welche Werke Beethovens fehlen in der Breitkopf & Härtelschen Gesamtausgabe?" *Neues Beethoven Jahrbuch*, 1937, with Supplement, 1939.
11. ——"Beethoven's Last Composition," *Music & Letters*, July, 1952.
12. Hoffman, E. T. A. *Sämtliche Schriften*, Vol. 15. Leipzig.

Bibliography

13. Kalischer, Alfred. *Beethovens Briefe.* Vol. III (1909-11), IV & V (1908).
14. ———*Neue Beethoven Briefe.* Berlin and Leipzig, 1902.
15. Kastner-Kapp. *Neue Beethoven Briefe* (new edition by Julius Kapp). 1923.
16. Kerst, Friedrich. *Die Erinnerungen an Beethoven. Vol.* I. 1913.
17. Klatte, Wilhelm. *Grundlagen des mehrstimmigen Satzes.* Berlin, 1922.
18. ———*Die moderne Theorie.* Berlin.
19. Leichtentritt, Hugo. *Musical Form.* Cambridge, 1951.
20. Leitzmann, Albert. *Beethovens Persönlichkeit.* 1914.
21. Lenz, Wilhelm von. *Beethoven, eine Kunststudie.* Hamburg, 1860.
22. Marx, A. B. *Ludwig van Beethoven, Leben und Schaffen.* Leipzig, 1859. 5th ed., 1901.
23. *Die Musik.* Fifth special Beethoven number.
24. ——— Tenth special Beethoven number (1912).
25. ——— Vol. 2, No. 3.
26. Nagel, Willibald. *Beethoven und seine Klaviersonaten.* Langensalza, 1924.
27. Nohl, Walther. *Ludwig van Beethovens Konversationshefte.* 1923.
28. Nottebohm, Martin. *Beethoveniana,* I and II.
29. ——— *Neue Beethoveniana.*
30. ——— *Ein Skizzenbuch von Beethoven.* Leipzig, 1865.
31. Prelinger, Fritz. *Ludwig van Beethovens sämtliche Briefe und Aufzeichnungen.* Vienna and Leipzig, 1907–11.
32. Riemann, Hugo. *Analyse der Beethoven Klaviersonaten mit historischen Notizen aesthetische und formaltechische Analyze.* Berlin, 1920.
33. ——— *Grundriss der Kompositionslehre.* Leipzig, 1910.
34. ——— *Musiklexikon.* Berlin, 1929.
35. Riezler, Walter. *Beethoven.* English translation, London.

36. San Galli, Thomas. *Ludwig van Beethoven.* Munich, 1913.

37. Schmitz, Arnold. *Das romantische Beethovenbild.* Berlin and Bonn, 1927.

38. Schünemann, Georg. "Neue Kanons von Beethoven," *Festschrift zu Arnold Scherings 60. Geburstag,* 1937.

39. Thayer, A. W. *Life of Ludwig van Beethoven.* (Krehbiel Edition.)

40.—— *Ludwig van Beethovens Leben* (translated by Deiters).
Vol. I, revised by Deiters, 1891.
Vols. II and III, revised by Riemann.
Vol. II, further revised by Riemann, 1919.
Vol. II, further revised by Riemann, 1919.
Vols. IV and V, written by Deiters from Thayer's material, edited by Riemann, 1907–1908.

41. Tovey, Donald. *The Main Stream of Music.* First printed in England in 1949 under the title, *Essays and Lectures on Music.*

42. Unger, Max. "Neue Beethoven Studien," *Neue Zeitschrift für Musik,* 1914.

43. —— "Zur Vieldeutigkeit von Beethovens Instrumentalmusik." *Schweizerische Musik-Zeitung* No. 14/15, 1937.

44. —— Catalogue of the Bodmer Beethoven Collection, 1939.

45. —— "Von ungedruckter Musik Beethovens." *Zeitschrift für Musik.* November, 1935.

46. —— *Beethoven und seine Verleger S. A.* Steiner und Tobias Haslinger in Wien.

47. Volkmann, Hans. *Beethoven als Epigrammatiker.* Published in (23).

48. Wasielewsky, Joseph von . . .*Ludwig van Beethoven.* Vol. II. 1888.

49. Wagner, Richard. *Sämtliche Schriften und Dichtungen.* Leipzig.

Index

Index

Index